Launch into Literacy

Book 4

Jane Medwell
Maureen Lewis

OXFORD
UNIVERSITY PRESS

Contents

There is no time limit on the sessions and teachers will want to exercise their own skill and judgement when planning

 = whole class work

NLS planning chart

	Genre focus	Range of texts	Text features	Reading skills

UNIT·1	TERM 1
	Writing to inform:
	  biographies and
	    autobiographies
		biography
		autobiography
		dictionaries
		atlas
		newspaper reports
			background
			  information
			chronological order
			key events
			facts and opinions
			conclusions
			newspaper reports
			recounts
				literal and inferential
				  comprehension
				implicit and explicit views
				using a range of
				  dictionaries
				using an atlas
				reading a time line

UNIT·2	TERM 1
	Writing to express:
	  playscripts and
	  poetry
		Macbeth
		narrative poems
			dialogue
			stage directions
			values and views in
			  literature
			paragraph structures
			similes and metaphors
				literal and inferential
				  comprehension
				rhythm, rhyme
				understanding early
				  modern English

UNIT·3	TERM 2
	Writing to entertain:
	  historical novels
		historical stories	treatment of time
			  (flashbacks)
			narrative opening
			images to create atmosphere
			paragraph structure
			similes and metaphors
			setting
			anthropomorphism
			point of view
				literal and inferential
				  comprehension
				dialect and standard
				  English
				evaluating the writer's
				  point of view

UNIT·4	TERM 2
	Writing to discuss:
	  discussion documents
		newspaper articles
		discussion texts
		headlines
		proverbs
		letters
			statement of issue
			arguments for
			arguments against
				reading explanations
				literal and inferential
				  comprehension
				questions
				facts and opinions
				using a dictionary

UNIT·5	TERM 3
	Writing to explain:
	  written explanations
		explanations
		leaflets
		lists
			statement + details
			technical vocabulary
			diagrams
				reading explanations
				literal and inferential
				  comprehension
				questions
				using a dictionary

Writing skills	Grammar	Punctuation	Word level

writing biography
brainstorming
setting questions
drafting
using paragraphs
revising writing
genre exchange: from
    biography to
       autobiography
writing a newspaper report
	first and third person
	proper nouns
	clauses
	past tense
		complex sentences
		commas
			word origins
			alphabetical order
			positive and negative
			    words
			definitions

writing poetry in a
    given form
drafting
revising
word order in sentences
writing a modern version
    of a classic text
	brackets, commas and
	    dashes for parentheses
		semi-colons
		colons
		commas
			rhyme, rhythm
			archaic words
			word order
			suffixes

writing a historical story planning drafting	active and passive verbs subject, agent clauses	semi-colons	vocabulary suffixes mnemonics old-fashioned words dialect and accent
writing a discussion writing headlines proverbs letters brainstorming drafting paragraphs revised writing	contrastive connectives conditional sentences modal verbs	laying out speech using appropriate marks to punctuate a letter	definitions inflated language persuasive words and phrases word play—puns
writing an explanation listing factors adding reasons creating causal sentences drafting revising writing writing a leaflet writing a slogan	causal conjunctions main clauses subordinate clauses complex sentences compound sentences past, present and future tense	punctuating complex sentences	creating new words alphabetical order anagrams palindromes pangrams lipograms definitions

Writing to inform

In this unit you will study how biographies and autobiographies are written. At the end of the unit you will plan, draft and write a biographical account of your own.

The Biography of Mary Seacole

Growing up in Kingston

background information on Mary's family

Mary was born in Kingston, Jamaica in 1805. Her mother had been a slave, from Africa, who had gained her freedom. She had worked hard growing vegetables on a small piece of land and had saved up enough money to buy an inn. At that time there were many British soldiers and sailors in Kingston. Mary's mother had married a Scottish officer. They had three children – Mary, Edward and Louisa.

Mary's mother had learned to use the herbs that grew in Jamaica to treat illnesses. She often looked after the British officers and their wives who stayed in Kingston. Mary often watched her mother looking after sick and wounded officers. By the time she was 12, she was helping her mother to treat her patients.

This implies she learnt from her mother

Travel and marriage

events in chronological order

When Mary was 12, she visited England with some of her relatives. She stayed in England for a year. She was called names by other children because she was black. Nonetheless, she went back to London many times. By the time she was 20, she had also been to other Caribbean islands to see what she could buy and sell.

- What is the purpose of this text?
- Who is telling these events?
- Why is prominence given to Mary's experiences as a nurse/doctor?
- Why are the links with Britain emphasized?
- Does this recount focus upon feelings or upon events?

In 1836, Mary met an English Officer called Horatio Edwin Seacole who was staying at her mother's inn. They fell in love and were married. Sadly, before long, he became very ill. Mary nursed him but he died. Soon afterwards Mary's mother died too.

mainly past tense

Blundell Hall, the inn run by Mrs Grant

information in illustrations as well as text

Helping the sick

Mary became well known as what the Jamaicans called a 'doctress'. The inn was always full of sick army officers. When army doctors stayed there Mary learned from them about medicine and surgery. When one woman died from cholera Mary helped the doctor. She found out as much as she could about this dreadful disease.

In 1850, Mary went to Panama where her brother Edward had opened a shop and a hotel. She took her medicine chest. While she was there, a friend of her brother became very ill and died within a few days. Mary knew that he had died of cholera. Many more people began to suffer from the same disease. There was no doctor and so they went to Mary for help. One night a baby, whom Mary had tried to save, died from cholera. She wanted to learn more about the disease and so she cut open the little body to examine it before burying it. Later she wrote that this helped her to understand cholera and to save other people's lives.

key events selected

third person pronouns

causal links between events

from *Mary Seacole* by Christine Moorcroft and Magnus Magnusson

UNIT·1 **Writing to inform**

Reading skills:
comprehension
Word level:
definitions
Grammar:
*third person to
first person*

Comprehension and vocabulary

1 Look again at the passage on pages 4 and 5.
Answer these questions.
  a Where was Mary born?
  b What was Mary's surname when
    she was a child?
  c What was her surname when she
    got married?
  d What evidence is there that Mary was
    a great traveller?
  e How did Mary learn about treating illnesses?
  f How did Mary get to know a lot about treating cholera?
  g What suggests that Mary might have written an
    autobiography (her own story of her life)?

Remember

You can use a
dictionary to
look up word
meanings.

2 Give a **definition** for the following words from the passage.
  a Freedom means
  b Surgery means
  c Herbs means
  d Examine means
  e 'Doctress' means

3 Read this and answer the question below.

*In 1854 I travelled from Jamaica to London once more. I wanted to use my
skills to help the soldiers who were getting wounded in the dreadful war between
Britain and Russia. I brought with me letters from several doctors, all of whom
praised my work. The War Office would not even look at them. They sent me away.*

Who do you think is writing this? How do you know?

4 Rewrite the first paragraph of Mary's **biography** as though it
was an **autobiography**. It has been started for you.

  I was born in Kingston...

Glossary

definition
biography
autobiography

5 Make a list of all the words you have changed in a grid.

Sentence	Word	Changed
1	Mary	I
2	her	my
3		

Words from Greek and Latin

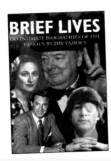 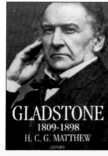 

In this unit we are looking at **biographies** and **autobiographies**. Both words are created by combining words that originate from ancient Greek (G) or Latin (L).

bio = life (G)   graph = written (G & L)   auto = self (L)

bio + graphy = life writing

auto + bio + graphy = self-life writing

Remember

An etymological dictionary tells us about word origins.

1 Here are some more words from Greek and Latin.

hydro = water (G)   aqua = water (L)
aero = air (G)   anti = against (G)
tele = far off (G) phobia = fear (G)

Use this information to try to work out the literal meaning of these words.

2 Compare your ideas with a partner's and then check in a dictionary.

Word	What I work it out to mean
hydroelectric	
hydrophobia	
autograph	
aqualung	
aeroplane	
aerosol	
anti-freeze	
television	
telegraph	

3 Add more words to each group.

bio	graph	auto	hydro	aqua	anti	tele	terra	phobia

Glossary
biography
autobiography

7

More word origins

1 Find two **proper nouns** for places and four proper nouns for people's names in the passage on pages 4 and 5.

> Mary was born in Kingston. 'Kingston' means the King's estate from the Middle English word 'toun' meaning estate. Many place names contain old words from other languages.
>
> EXAMPLES:
>
> Grimsby – "by" – Viking word means farmstead
> Bideford – "ford" – Old English word means river crossing

2 Use an atlas of Britain to find three place names which end with each of these old words from another language.

ton (estate)
by (farmstead)
ham (homestead)
bury (manor house)
well (spring or stream)

Remember
You could check the origin of the word in a dictionary of place names.

Mary became a popular name because it occurs in the Bible. Edward is an Old English word meaning happiness or prosperity. Names can come from different countries, languages and times in history.

3 Arrange these names in alphabetical order. You may need to look at the second and third letters to get the order correct.

Karen Alan Kylie Almira Kismet Winston
Kevin Wendy Ann Alfred Winifred Kerry Keith

Glossary
proper noun

4 Do some research, using dictionaries of names, to discover the meaning and origin of the names.

Facts and opinions

Facts are statements that can be shown to be true.
Opinions are what people think.

> Manchester United are a football team.

Fact

> Manchester United are the greatest.

Opinion

> Manchester United are rubbish.

Opinion

1 Read these two brief accounts of Mary's life.

An Extraordinary Life

Born in 1802 to a Jamaican hotelier and a Scottish army officer, Mary Seacole spent her childhood with British military men who she greatly admired. A brief marriage ended in her husband's death but left her wealthy. She visited England and Central America where she set up a string of hotels and prospected for gold.

She learned both western medicine and West Indian herbal remedies, was a skilled surgeon and gained experience nursing cholera and yellow fever victims.

When newspaper reports of British troops suffering from cholera and typhus in the Crimea reached her in Jamaica, she was determined to help in any way she could.

From *Tales of Real Heroism* by Paul Dowswell

A Dedicated Nurse

A Jamaican woman named Mary Seacole (1805-81) became a nurse in 1850, during an outbreak of a disease called cholera. A few years later she sailed to England to offer her services as a Crimean War nurse, but was turned down because she was black.

Undeterred, Mary paid for her own passage to the Crimea and spent the next three years working with Florence Nightingale, providing medical care for the war casualties.

When she returned to England, Mary was praised for her bravery by the same people who had previously rejected her help.

from *Famous Women from Nefertiti to Thatcher* by Richard Dungworth and Philippa Wingate

2 Now write 'fact' or 'opinion' against each of the sentences below. If the accounts disagree write 'needs checking'.

  a Mary was born in 1802.

  b Mary was a skilled nurse.

  c Mary's offer to help in the war was turned down.

  d Mary was rejected because she was black.

3 Use the information above and on pages 4 and 5.

  a Write three facts about Mary Seacole.

  b Write three opinions about Mary Seacole.

UNIT·1 **Writing to inform**

Reading skills:
comprehension
Word level:
*positive and
negative words*

Implicit and explicit views

1 Reread the two accounts of Mary on the previous page.

2 What word in each **title** shows that the authors thought Mary was a special person?

3 In 'A Dedicated Nurse' what do you think is the author's opinion of the people who turned Mary away? What makes you think this?

4 What do the words 'determined' and 'undeterred' make you think about Mary's character?

5 Do the authors explicitly say they admire Mary? If not, how do you know that they admired her?

> The choice of words can influence what we think about a person. EXAMPLE: *Determined* implies a person does not give up easily but *stubborn* would imply they would not give up even if it were sensible to do so.

6 Read this passage.

> The king was a <u>tall</u>, <u>handsome</u> man with <u>broad</u> shoulders and an <u>impressive</u> manner. He had a voice that was <u>gentle</u> and <u>calm</u> although when he was angry it had a steely note.
> He was determined his orders should be followed for they were <u>fair</u> and <u>just</u>. Wherever he went his people cheered for they loved him greatly.

Some of the words which make you feel positive about the character have been underlined. Find another four positive words.

gentle

7 Now rewrite the passage replacing the positive words with negative words, e.g. 'weak' for 'gentle'.

8 Discuss the impact of the changes.

Glossary

title

Punctuation of complex sentences

In Book 3 you looked at some rules for punctuating complex sentences. Here are the rules again.

If the subordinate clause or phrase comes at the beginning of the sentence, it is separated from the main clause by a comma.

1 Find an example of this kind of sentence. Read the 'Travel and marriage' section of The Biography of Mary Seacole on page 4.

If the subordinate clause or phrase splits the main clause, it is marked by commas.

2 Find an example of this kind of sentence. Read the 'Growing up in Kingston' section of The Biography of Mary Seacole on page 4.

If the main clause comes first, a comma is not needed to mark the subordinate clause or phrase.

3 Find an example of this kind of sentence. Read the 'Growing up in Kingston' section of The Biography of Mary Seacole on page 4.

4 Add a subordinate clause to each of these simple sentences. Make sure you also add any extra punctuation that is needed.
   a Mary was born in Jamaica.
   b Her mother ran a hotel.
   c Mary travelled to other countries.
   d Mary could use West Indian herbal medicines.

Glossary
subordinate clause
main clause

11

Mary Seacole

Here is a further section of Mary Seacole's biography.

background information

Determined to help, Seacole had contacted a London relative, Thomas Day, and set up a trading company with him. The firm of 'Seacole and Day' was set up, provisions were purchased and the two had set sail for the Crimea, landing at Balaclava in early 1855.

third person pronouns

For the first six weeks Seacole sold supplies from the quayside. For her protection she carried a pistol in the belt around her waist. She looked after the wounded whenever she could and at night slept aboard the supply ship Medura. This was loaded with gunpowder and those on board were in constant danger of instant annihilation from a fire or a stray shell.

events in chronological order

After a couple of months Seacole and Day managed to build a small collection of huts close to Balaclava which they called 'The British Hotel'. It was a great success and Seacole soon became well known to many of the soldiers. Aside from a warm welcome and the medical attention she provided Seacole's cooking was unusually good.

Life was still extraordinarily difficult. The Crimean winter was bitterly cold. Valuable supplies were swept away in a flash flood. Thieving was a constant problem and rats ate supplies and nibbled at sleeping hotel staff.

Despite all her problems, Seacole was not distracted from her work.

implied information

key events selected

She not only nursed soldiers at the hotel and at the local field hospital, she also went out to the battlefield. Nursing so near the fighting required an iron nerve. After heavy fighting the ground would be thick with wounded men, often horribly mutilated. Some called urgently for her attention. Others, crazy with pain, tugged desperately at her clothing as she passed. Anyone who needed attention, whether friend or foe, was given it.

mainly past tense

from *Tales of Real Heroism* by Paul Dowswell

1 Look carefully at the passage and then answer these questions.
   a When and where did Seacole arrive in the Crimea?
   b Who set up in business with Mary Seacole?
   c Why did Mary carry a pistol?

   d What was dangerous about sleeping on board the ship?
   e What three things made 'the British Hotel' well known.
   f Give three reasons why life was difficult.
   g What was Mary Seacole's main purpose for being in the Crimea?

2 Give a **definition** for the following words from the passage.
   a Provisions means
   b Quayside means
   c Constant means

Remember
You can use a dictionary to look up word meanings.

   d Distracted means
   e Annihilation means

3 This extract is from a book called *Tales of Real Heroism*. Do you think Mary Seacole deserves to be written about under this title? Give reasons for your answer.

Glossary
definition

Starting in the middle

Most **biographies** and **autobiographies** start at the beginning of someone's life and work through in order. However, some jump straight into a piece of dramatic action as a way of gaining the reader's attention.

1 Read the opening of 'Mother Seacole's Balaclava Boys'. This author has started with a dramatic event.

In the winter of 1855, at the height of the Crimean War, the Russian town of Balaclava could have been anyone's idea of hell. It was here that wounded and diseased soldiers from the nearby siege of Sebastopol assembled to be taken to special hospitals a safe distance from the fighting.

Some sat uncomplaining on hillside or horseback, their dull eyes glazed in misery. Others, with bloody bandages covering disfiguring wounds, lay on stretchers, writhing in agony. Amid the chaos dying men called desperately for attention. Along this grim procession strode an unlikely figure in a yellow dress and blue bonnet, dispensing medicine, food and encouragement. Many of the soldiers recognized this plump middle-aged Jamaican woman. She was Mary Seacole.

from *Tales of Real Heroism* by Paul Dowswell

2 Choose one of these dramatic events.
- Mary's first visit to London aged 12.
- The death of her husband.
- Nursing cholera victims in Panama.
- Being turned away from the War Office in London.

3 Use the event to write the opening of Mary's biography. Use information and your imagination.

'The young woman looked at the small, dead baby. The dreaded cholera had claimed another victim.'

4 Now rewrite your paragraph in the first person as though Mary herself was the author.

I gazed down at the small, dead baby. The dreaded cholera had claimed another victim. I felt...

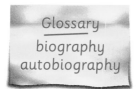

UNIT·1 Writing
to inform

Text features:
conclusions,
newspaper reports
Reading skills:
reading a
time line,
comprehension

Closing a biography

Here is the closing section of 'Mother Seacole's Balaclava Boys'.

With the fall of the city the war was almost over and troops began to leave. Although she had succeeded in her aim of nursing the soldiers, Seacole's British Hotel had become a financial disaster. The Jamaican nurse was deep in debt.

Seacole left the Crimea for London by steam boat, arriving bankrupt but a heroine, some months later. The very fact that she had made no profit from her hotel when others with similar stores had made fortunes, made her even more appreciated by the British press and public. On the streets of London she was constantly stopped and thanked by soldiers who recognized her .

"Wherever I go," she wrote, "I am sure to meet some smiling face."

from *Tales of Real Heroism* by Paul Dowswell

This is what happened to Mary after the war.

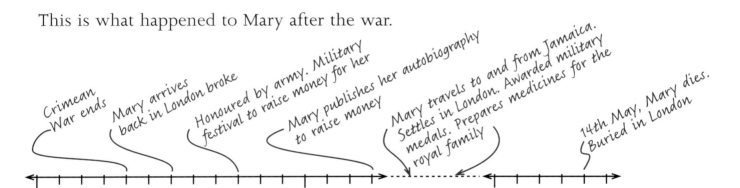

1 Answer these questions using the passage and the time line.
   a When did Mary return to London?
   b Why was Mary short of money?
   c How was money raised for her?
   d How did Mary make money for herself?
   e What was Mary's **autobiography** called?
   f How do we know people appreciated Mary's work?

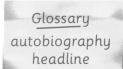

2 Make up a newspaper headline about Mary being short of money. Then write a brief newspaper report to go with your **headline**.

Crimean heroine living in poverty
Soldiers of this country have reason to be grateful to Mary Seacole.....

Glossary
autobiography
headline

Writing a biographical account

You have looked at several different biographies of Mary Seacole in this unit. Now you are going to write your own biographical piece about a friend.

1 Look at the passages you have studied in this unit.

2 Decide who you are going to write about.

3 Brainstorm a list of questions you need to ask them based on a grid your teacher will give you.

Brainstorm

Topic	Questions
Family background	How many brothers/sisters/ages? Who else in family? Where born? Where living?
Personality, interests, clubs, etc.	
Life before school	
Life in the infants	
Life in the juniors	
3 key events in life so far	
Plans and hopes for the future	

4 Interview your subject and make notes on each answer.

5 Use each grid heading as a new paragraph or section. Write a first draft of each section using the information in your notes.

6 Look at your choice of words. Are they positive or negative?

7 Decide on the order of the sections: background, introduction and chronological events or starting with a dramatic moment?

8 Decide on any illustrations, fact boxes needed.

9 Create a draft.

10 Discuss your draft with a friend and make any necessary amendments.

11 Complete a final version of the biography.

Plan

Draft

Revise

Publish

Writing to express

In this unit you are going to study some classic poetry and drama. You will examine how plays are presented and how scripts can be used effectively.

brief description of the scene

information about what happens on stage

Act 4

Scene I A cave on the moor. In the centre is a boiling cauldron

Thunder. *Enter the three Witches.*

FIRST WITCH:	Thrice the brinded cat hath mew'd.
SECOND WITCH:	Thrice and once the hedge-pig whin'd.
THIRD WITCH:	Harpier cries: 'Tis time, 'tis time.
FIRST WITCH:	Round about the cauldron go;
	In the poison'd entrails throw. 5
	Toad, that under cold stone
	Days and nights hast thirty-one
	Swelter'd venom, sleeping got,
	Boil thou first i' the charmed pot.
ALL:	Double, double, toil and trouble; 10
	Fire burn and cauldron bubble.
SECOND WITCH:	Fillet of a fenny snake,
	In the cauldron boil and bake;
	Eye of newt, and toe of frog,
	Wool of bat, and tongue of dog, 15
	Adder's fork, and blind-worm's sting,
	Lizard's leg, and howlet's wing,
	For a charm of powerful trouble,
	Like a hell-broth boil and bubble.

names of the speakers are on the left-hand side of the page

This is an extract from Shakespeare's play *Macbeth*.
The play is a story of murder, greed and power.
It is set in Scotland.

- Are the witches young, old, male or female?
- How do the witches move?
- What is the setting of the scene like?
- What objects would you need to use to stage this scene of the play?

ALL:	Double, double, toil and trouble; Fire burn and cauldron bubble.	20
THIRD WITCH:	Scale of dragon, tooth of wolf, Witches' mummy, maw and gulf Of the ravin'd salt-sea shark, Root of hemlock digg'd i' the dark, Liver of blaspheming Jew, Gall of goat, and slips of yew Sliver'd in the moon's eclipse, Nose of Turk, and Tartar's lips, Finger of birth-strangled babe Ditch-deliver'd by a drab, Make the gruel thick and slab; Add thereto a tiger's chaudron, For the ingredients of our cauldron.	25 30
ALL:	Double, double, toil and trouble; Fire burn and cauldron bubble.	35
SECOND WITCH:	Cool it with a baboon's blood, Then the charm is firm and good.	

the words spoken by the characters written without speech marks

fenny – slimy
harpier – name of a familiar, a witch's evil creature
swelter'd venom – poisonous sweat
maw and gulf – stomach and throat
ravin'd – full of devoured prey
drab – prostitute
slab – sticky
chaudron – entrails

footnotes to help the reader

from *Macbeth* by William Shakespeare (1564–1616)

Remember

Try to imagine
how the play
would look
when acted out.

Remember

Use a dictionary
(or etymological
dictionary) to
find old words.

Comprehension and vocabulary

1 Reread the extract on pages 18 and 19.

2 Now answer these questions.
   a The witches are
      having a party?
      brewing a spell?
      cooking a meal?
   b The passage is
      a list?
      a playscript?
      a report?

   c Thrice means
      three times?
      already?
      some time ago?
   d Write out the meaning of the following words:
      brinded
      gruel
      entrails

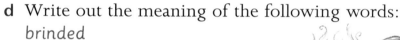

   e How is the toad described?

   f Write out the chorus or refrain which is chanted by
      all the witches together.
   g The chorus is
      a couplet?   *a rhyme?*   *a poem?*

3 What are the witches doing as they chant this piece?

4 Do you think this is a good or bad spell?
   Justify your opinion.

5 Write a sentence to summarise the action in this passage.

Views and attitudes in literature

Macbeth was written by William Shakespeare in 1606.
Beliefs and attitudes have changed since that time.
Read the following extracts.

Witchcraft was recognised in English law of Shakespeare's time; it was punishable by death. The King of England, King James, was interested in the subject and in 1597 wrote a pamphlet about witchcraft. A few years earlier, the King himself had been the victim of a witches' plot. A witch confessed to having tried to poison the king using poison from a toad. Although people did recognise that some witchcraft was the result of trickery, belief in the power of witches was widespread.

from *Shakespeare's Day* by Jane Medwell (2000)

1 What happened to people found guilty of witchcraft in Shakespeare's day?

2 Why was the King's attitude to witchcraft important?

3 What would the original audience for Shakespeare's *Macbeth* have thought about witches?

A Modern Witch
by William Oxley

I'm a modern witch
A modern witch do you hear?
I don't ride on a switch, a broom or a stick
I ride on a rocket
With spells in my pocket
And things electronic
For I'm a new kind of witch
A modern witch do you hear?

I'm a modern witch
A modern witch do you hear?
I still use spells
And my cauldron smells
But I'm no hag
No silly old bag
Who lags behind the times –
For I'm a modern witch
A very modern witch indeed.

4 How do you know the poem on the right is modern?

5 Whose voice is heard in the poem?

6 In the poem, what sort of character is the witch?
Give evidence for your views.

7 Describe how attitudes to witchcraft have changed since Shakespeare's day.

Remember
Use a dictionary and an encyclopaedia to find information you need

Old words, old views

1 Write out the ingredients of the witches' spell (pages 18–19) in modern language.

Spell ingredients
intestines
poisonous toad
magic pot
slimy snake

The natural and biological items listed above are all included in the witches' spell because Shakespeare's audience would have seen them as evil. However, we now know toads, for example, are not poisonous and do a useful job of insect control.

2 Complete the table to show how modern views of these species have changed.

Organism	What is it?	How do we see it now?	Why might Shakespeare have believed it was evil?
hedge-pig			
blind-worm	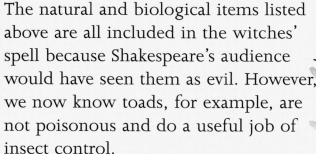		Looks like a snake and so might be poisonous.
yew			
howlet	A baby owl	Harmless. Hunts mice and small animals at night. Some types are protected by law.	

Old words fall out of use but are often replaced by new ones.

3 Look up the meaning of these words and write down the modern equivalent:
 • yonder
 • hence
 • hither

4 List three words which have come into use recently (such as computer).

Poetic language

UNIT·2 Writing
to express

Sentence
features:
*word order,
rhythm, rhyme*

> The witches' speech is written in verse (poetry) with a
> strong **rhythm** and **rhyme**. **Word order** is very important
> for the rhythm and rhyme of the poetry.

1   Rewrite these passages as sentences, using the same words
    but putting them in a more usual order.

    EXAMPLE: Thrice the brinded cat hath mewed.
                The brinded cat hath mewed thrice.

    a Round about the cauldron go;
        In the poisoned entrails throw.
    b Toad, that under cold stone
        Days and nights hath thirty-one
        Sweltered venom sleeping got
        Boil thou first i' the charmed pot.
    c Thrice and once the hedge-pig whined.

2   What is the effect on the rhyme of changing word order?

3   Rewrite this passage as an ordinary sentence. Use the
    original words but change some of the features of
    poetry, including:
    • the capital letters at the beginning of lines
    • the order of the words
    • the way the lines are set out
    • extra words which give the piece rhythm.

    In the cauldron boil and bake;
    Eye of newt, and toe of frog,
    Wool of bat, and tongue of dog,
    Adder's fork, and blind-worm's sting,
    Lizard's leg, and howlet's wing,
    For a charm of powerful trouble,
    Like a hell-broth boil and bubble.

4   What happens to the rhythm of the piece when you make it
    into an ordinary sentence?

Glossary
rhythm
rhyme

UNIT·2 Writing to express

Writing skills:
*writing poetry in
a given form,
drafting, revising*

Writing a spell

This is your chance to write a spell in a similar form to the witches' spell on pages 18 and 19.

1 Reread the witches' spell on pages 18 and 19.

2 Choose what sort of spell you would like to write and write out your title.

A spell to turn all food into chocolate
A spell to fly me to Florida
A spell to turn Jerry's hair green

3 Assemble a list of ingredients for your spell. They should be suitable for the type of spell you want to produce.

A spell to turn all food into chocolate
Super sweet sugar
Melting moments

4 Think of any actions you want to include in your spell and make a note of them.

5 Write a chorus for your spell as two lines which rhyme: a rhyming couplet.

6 Draft your spell as a poem with a rhythm like the one on pages 18 and 19 which has four beats.

7 When you have your draft, discuss it with a partner.
Ask yourselves:
  • Are the ingredients of the spell interesting?
  • Does the spell have a pattern of rhymes?
  • Does the chorus go well with the rest of the spell?
  • Does the rhythm of the spell make you want to chant it?

8 Mark any changes to your spell on the draft.

Colons, commas and semi-colons

A **colon** can be used to precede a list of words, phrases or clauses.

In the cauldron boil and bake:
Eye of newt and toe of frog,
Wool of bat and tongue of dog.

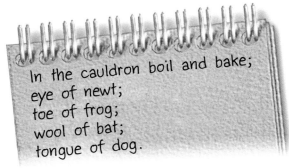

In the cauldron boil and bake;
eye of newt;
toe of frog;
wool of bat;
tongue of dog.

1 Rewrite these sentences, putting in the colon before the list and **commas** between the items.

Remember
Do not use a comma before the final 'and' or 'but'

   a Go to the magic shop and buy sparkle powder fake blood dried bat's droppings and toad cubes.

   b This spell requires a dog's tooth two bats' wings some cat's hair and a sour lemon.

   c I want to change the weather my hair colour Maggie's opinion of me and the teacher's personality.

   d This spell works on nice people bus drivers doctors caretakers but not teachers.

Where the items in the list are phrases or clauses, a **semi-colon** can be used after the colon to separate items in the list. A semi-colon is a 'stronger' separation between items in a list than a comma. It is not used when the items in a list are only one or two words long.

2 Rewrite this passage as a list.

Walter the wizard thought of the three terrible things that had happened to him that day: he had been caught faking a spell to charm frogs; he had been dragged before the wizard's court and exposed as a fraud to his colleagues; his wizard licence had been ceremoniously taken from him and torn up. It had been the worst day of his life!

Glossary
phrase
clause
comma

3 Rewrite the passage as five separate sentences.

Macbeth meets the witches

You are now going to study a further extract from *Macbeth*, in which Macbeth meets the witches.

cont. is an abbreviation of continued

ACT 4
Scene I *(cont.)*

SECOND WITCH:	By the pricking of my thumbs,	45
	Something wicked this way comes.	
	Open, locks,	
	Whoever knocks.	

Enter MACBETH

stage direction

MACBETH:	How now, you secret, black, and midnight hags!
	What is't you do?

ALL:	A deed without a name.	
MACBETH:	I conjure you, by that which you profess, –	50
	Howe'er you come to know it – answer me:	
	Though you untie the winds and let them fight	
	Against the churches; though the yesty waves	
	Confound and swallow navigation up;	
	Though bladed corn be lodg'd and trees blown down;	55
	Though castles topple on their warders' heads;	
	Though palaces and pyramids do slope	
	Their heads to their foundations; though the treasure	
	Of Nature's germens tumble all together,	
	Even till destruction sicken; answer me	6
	To what I ask you.	

Macbeth commands the witches

repeated to strengthen the order

yesty – frothy
navigation – ships
bladed corn be lodged – the corn flattened in the fields
warders – owners, keepers
slope – bend
Nature's germens – the seeds of all life

UNIT·2 Writing to express

Text features: *comprehension*
Reading skills: *rhythm, rhyme*
Writing skills: *transforming old words into modern language*

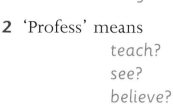

1 'Conjure you' means
    order you?
    trick you?
    magic?

2 'Profess' means
    teach?
    see?
    believe?

3 Write out 'howe'er' in full.

4 Macbeth demands that the witches
    make a spell for him?
    answer his questions?
    go away?

5 What is Macbeth's opinion of the witches?

6 How do you think Macbeth feels about talking to the witches?

7 How is the rhythm of the witches' spell different from Macbeth's speech?

8 When is rhyme used?

9 Write out Macbeth's speech in modern language.

Using semi-colons

A **semi-colon** can be used to separate two **clauses** of equal weight in a **sentence**. It is often used in place of 'and' or of a full stop.

EXAMPLE: I prefer to drink tea; Maureen usually drinks coffee.

1 Write out the following sentences including semi-colons and any other punctuation you need.

   a The heat of the day seemed endless soon a breeze must come.

   b I went shopping for a dress I bought two pairs of trousers.

   c Brittany wanted earrings her mother had other ideas.

   d Sometimes Sam is my best friend at other times he practically ignores me.

2 Choose pairs of clauses from the list and join them with semi-colons to make three sentences.

it was a dark but silvery night
it was a terrible, dark, cold night
the moon shed an eerie light
the glen was totally silent
the night seemed cold and dead
a perfect night for witches

3 Punctuate the passage below.

The night had been perfect as dark as deep water with a clear sky What more could a beginner wizard want However even with such a perfect night none of the other wizards had turned up Walter was all on his own worse still he had no idea why his summoning spell had failed Walter was beginning to suspect he would never become a fully trained wizard

Glossary
clause
sentence
semi-colon

Parenthesis – adding explanation

A phrase or clause inserted into a sentence to make the meaning clearer is called **parenthesis**. The word or phrase can be separated from the rest of the sentence using **commas**, **dashes** or **brackets**.

EXAMPLES: The ducks (all green) were swimming quietly.
Sally, the oldest girl, was tired out.

My house – the old one – was right next to the school.

1 Use dashes or brackets to punctuate these sentences.
  a The cat a black one was useless at catching mice.
  b Walter's first and only spell was a disaster.
  c The war like all wars was terrible and bloody.
  d Poetry or most of it is a way of expressing thought.

2 Use commas, dashes or brackets to punctuate this passage.

At last it seemed a long time Walter had found a book about witchcraft. He opened it immediately and saw to his dismay a totally incomprehensible page. His luck as usual was bad and the book the only one he could get was in a language he couldn't read.

3 Parenthesis is often used in **playscripts** to tell the reader what a **character** does or how an action or speech is performed. Fill in the parentheses in the following script.

Cast – WALTER – a novice wizard
    HIGH WIZARD – Chairman of the Wizards' Council

HIGH WIZARD: (*sighs*) Well, Walter? You'd better tell me (*shakes head*).
Start at the beginning.
WALTER: (   ) I was just trying to do a simple spell.
    (   ) I'm sorry, you see…
HIGH WIZARD: (   ) Just get on with it, Walter.
No excuses.
WALTER: (   ) I found this spell on the internet.
    (   ) I thought that, just this once, I thought
    I could have a go.
HIGH WIZARD: (   ) And? And what exactly happened?
WALTER: (   ) Well, instead of raining it sort of.
    Well, it snowed.
HIGH WIZARD: In July. (   ) Enough, Walter.
Enough is enough.

Glossary
comma
dash
bracket
playscript
character

29

Writing a modern version of a poem

You are going to read a poem about how Edynfed, King of Dyfed, and his men were killed and then rewrite it in modern language.

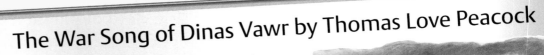

The War Song of Dinas Vawr by Thomas Love Peacock

The mountain sheep are sweeter,
But the valley sheep are fatter;
We therefore deemed it meeter,
To carry off the latter.
We made an expedition;
We met a host and quelled it;
We forced a strong position,
And killed the men who held it.

On Dyfed's richest valley,
Where herds of kine were browsing,
We made a mighty sally,
To finish our carousing.
Fierce warriors rushed to meet us;
We met them and o'erthrew them:
They struggled hard to beat us;
But we conquered them and slew them.

As we drove our prize at leisure,
The king marched forth to catch us;
His rage surpassed all measure,
But his people could not match us.
He fled to his hall pillars;
And, ere our force we led off,

Plan

1 Read the poem aloud to yourself. What words would you use to describe the poem?

2 Read each verse and make a note of what you think each verse is about.

3 Make a list of any words you do not know. Look them up in a thesaurus, dictionary or etymological dictionary and note what they mean.

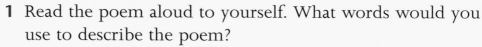

quelled – beat, overcame
sally – rush
slew – killed

4 Now check each verse of the poem again and write a summary of what happens in each verse.

Revise

Some sacked his house and cellars,
While others cut his head off.

We there, in strife bewildering,
Spilt blood enough to swim in;
We orphaned many children,
And widowed many women.
The eagles and the ravens
We glutted with our foemen:
The heroes and the cravens,
The spearmen and the bowmen.

We brought away from battle,
And much their land bemoaned them,
Two thousand head of cattle,
And the head of him who owned them:
Edynfed, King of Dyfed,
His head was borne before us;
His wine and beasts supplied our feasts,
And his overthrow, our chorus.

host – large group of people
kine – cows
sally – sudden attack on an enemy
carousing – drinking a lot of alcohol and making a lot of noise
glutted – fed to the point where they could eat no more
cravens – cowards

5 Write the poem out so that you retell each verse, with description, in prose.

6 Read the poem with a partner and discuss it using the following points:
  • The poem is in the first person plural (we).
    Have you used 'we' in your retelling?
  • Does the poem make the order of events clear?
  • Does the description tell the reader about the beauty and riches of the place as well as the horror of the battle?

  Mark any changes on your draft.

7 Make a final copy of your retelling.

Draft

Publish

31

Writing to entertain

In this unit you are going to study some extracts from historical novels set during wartime. You will pay particular attention to how the authors handle time in the stories and how the reader knows time is passing.

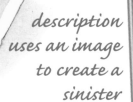

Chapter 1

Carrie had often dreamed about coming back. In her dreams she was twelve years old again; short, scratched legs in red socks and scuffed, brown sandals, walking along the narrow, dirt path at the side of the railway line to where it plunged down, off the high ridge, through the Druid's Grove. The yew trees in the Grove were dark green and so old that they had grown twisted and lumpy, like arthritic fingers. And in Carrie's dream, the fingers reached out for her, plucking at her hair and her skirt as she ran. She was always running by the end of this dream, running away from the house, uphill towards the railway line.

✧

But when she did come back, with her own children, the railway line had been closed. The sleepers had been taken up and the flat, stony top of the ridge was so overgrown with blackberries and wild rose and hazelnut bushes that it was like pushing through a forgotten forest in a fairy tale. The tangled wood round Sleeping Beauty's castle. Pulling off the sticky brambles that clung to their jeans, Carrie's children said, "No one's been here for hundreds of years ..."

"Not hundreds, *thousands* ..."

description uses an image to create a sinister atmosphere

what does this indicate?

language echoes first sentence of previous paragraph

description uses an image to create a harmless atmosphere

the speaker's thoughts about changes, rather than a description

UNIT·3 Writing to entertain

Text features:
*flashback,
narrative opening*
Setting:
*images to create
atmosphere*

- This is a historical novel. Does this mean the story is true?
- How is the atmosphere of the place different in the dream and in reality?
- What happens in Carrie's dream?
- What do you think the novel is going to be about?

time is discussed

"A hundred, thousand years. A million, billion, trillion ..."

"Only about thirty," Carrie said. She spoke as if this was no time at all. "I was here, with Uncle Nick, thirty years ago. During the war – when England was at war with Germany. The Government sent the children out of the cities so they shouldn't be bombed. We weren't told where we were going. Just told to turn up at our schools with a packed lunch and a change of clothes, then we went to the station with our teachers. There were whole train-loads of children sent away like that ..."

"Without their mummies?" the little ones said. "Without their dads?"

"Oh, quite alone," Carrie said. "I was eleven when we first came here. And Uncle Nick was going on ten."

Uncle Nick was old. He had been old for years and grown so fat in the stomach that he puffed when he stooped. The thought of him being ten years old made the children want to giggle but they bit the giggles back. Their mother was looking so strange: eyes half closed and dreaming. They looked at her pale, dreaming face and said nothing.

from *Carrie's War* by Nina Bawden

UNIT·3 Writing to entertain

Text level:
comprehension
Word level:
*vocabulary,
suffixes*

Comprehension and vocabulary

1 Reread the extract on pages 32 and 33.

2 Now answer these questions.
   a The setting of the story is

   a hill near a railway?   a house near a wooded
   railway line?   a station?

   b The main characters in the story are

   young children?   Carrie and her brother Nick?
   Uncle Nick and Mum?

   c Carrie comes back after

   thirty years?   several years?   hundreds of years?

3 a About how old is Carrie?
   b Why did the children feel like giggling?
   c Why did the children resist the temptation to giggle?
   d What happened to Carrie and Nick during the war?
   e How do you think Carrie felt when she thought of being
        sent away during the war?

4 *Carrie's War* is a historical novel. This means that

   the story actually happened as it is written?
   the story is set against events which did happen?
   the author has made up all the history in the story?

5 Write a **definition** of each of these words.
   a evacuee
   b evacuate
   c train
   d trainee
   c escape
   d escapee

6 The **suffix** -ee means

7 Use a suffix to change these verbs into the name for people
   who do the verb.

   perform reform   **explore** shop **buy** repair

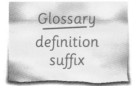

Glossary
definition
suffix

34

Setting

Text features:
paragraph structure, revising similes and metaphors

1 Reread the extract on pages 32 and 33.

2 The setting of the story is described in two ways –
   pick out the words and phrases which make the setting seem
   a sinister.
   b harmless.

3 a Read the second **paragraph** from *Carrie's War* on page 32.
   b Why had the place changed?
   c What were the two main changes?

4 Think of your classroom or school as it is now and what it is
   like at the begining of the school year, just before term
   starts. Make a list of adjectives and adjective phrases which
   describe the classroom now and then.

> **Remember**
> Similes often use 'like' or 'as . . .as' to compare something with something else.

THEN	NOW
gloomy	humming with activity
eerily empty	busy
	colourful

5 In the second paragraph on page 32 the writer compares the
   stony ridge with a forgotten forest in a fairy tale. Write a
   simile to describe your classroom or school.

6 In this paragraph the writer says the stony ridge is a tangled
   wood around Sleeping Beauty's castle. Write a **metaphor**
   for your classroom.

7 Now use this paragraph from *Carrie's War* as a model to help
   you write a paragraph to describe how your classroom has
   changed since the beginning of term.

The walls had been completely changed.

> **Remember**
> Write as if another person who knows your memories is telling the description.

> *Glossary*
> paragraph
> simile
> metaphor

Structuring paragraphs

1 This paragraph from Chapter 1 of *Carrie's War* describes what happened beside the railway, rather than what it looked like.

> Carrie said, "Nick and I used to walk from the town along the side of the railway. It was quite safe, not like an electrified line, and there weren't many trains, anyway. Only two or three a day and they came dead slow round the bend in case there were sheep on the track. When there were, the engine driver would stop the train and get out of his cab and shoo them off, and sometimes he'd wait so that everyone could get down from the carriages and stretch their legs and pick blackberries before they set off again. Nick and I never saw that, but people said it often happened. They were specially good blackberries here, easy to reach and not dusty, like at the side of a road. When they were ripe, Nick and I used to pick some to eat on the way."

2 Carrie talks about the railway line of the past in such a way that the reader notices the difference between that railway and modern railways. Complete the chart.

What Carrie says:	The change implied by what is said:
"It was safe, not like an electrified line."	
"There weren't many trains."	
The trains "came dead slow…in case there were sheep on the track."	
People could get out to "pick blackberries".	

3 Where else has Carrie collected blackberries, as well as beside the railway?

4 The **paragraph** above is Carrie's memory of the railway line. How accurate do you think the description was? Was the railway always like this?

5 Think of somewhere you walk quite often.
   a Make brief notes of two things you pass.
   b Make a note of something someone has told you about the place.
   c Write a paragraph like the one above, describing the place in terms of your memories.

Boon Hua Li and I used to go past the old swimming pool all the time. It was really chilly and dirty, not at all like a modern indoor swimming pool …

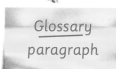

Glossary
paragraph

Active and passive verbs

1 Change the following sentences from active to passive.
   a The villagers looked after the children.
   b During the war, families grew food.
   c Gardeners water the vegetables regularly.
   d She picked up the basket of food.
   e The butcher sold meat to everyone.
   f The photographer took pictures of the party.
   g The whole village celebrated the end of the war.

> The **agent** in a sentence is the person or thing performing the action. EXAMPLE: <u>The</u> <u>dog</u> bit the man. (active)

2 Identify the agent in each of the sentences in 1 above.

> Sometimes 'by' is put in before the agent in **passive sentences** or the agent is not identified.
> EXAMPLE: The man was bitten <u>by</u> the dog. or
> The man was bitten.

3 Say whether there is an agent or not for each of these sentences.
   a The lemonade was completely used up.
   b The guns were silenced for the memorial service.
   c The fizzy drink was consumed by Ben.
   d The marrows were eaten by slugs.
   e The cauliflowers were totally ruined.

4 Rewrite this passage using passive sentences to make it sound more formal.

The army men found a bomb in Gary's garden. The Germans dropped it on London, but missed the target. The bomb disposal men arrived very quickly. They examined the bomb and declared a danger zone. The notices said DANGER UXB. The excitement thrilled Gary.

> Glossary
> agent
> passive

37

Goodnight Mister Tom

You are now going to study an extract from *Goodnight Mister Tom* by Michelle Magorian. This book is about a child, William Beach, who was evacuated to the countryside during the Second World War and lived with Tom Oakley.

direct speech

setting

Tom's feelings

Willie's feelings

"On market days that be filled with all kinds of stalls," said Tom.

In the centre of the square was a stone archway with a clock in its wall and on the ground below, surrounding it on four sides, were wooden benches.

They stopped outside a newsagent's shop. Two placards were leaning up against the wall. 'Poland invaded!' read one and 'Turn your wireless low. Remember, someone might be on duty,' read the other. The door of the shop was already propped wide open.

"Hot, ent it?" said a tiny old lady from behind the counter. "Your usual is it, Mr Oakley?" she added.

Tom nodded.

She reached up to a yellow tin of tobacco on one of the shelves. A pile of comics caught Willie's eye. Tom glanced at him.

"One sweet and one comic," he said sharply. "Choose."

Willie was stunned.

"Don't you hurry, sonny," said the old lady kindly. "You jest takes yer time." She pointed up at some of the many jars. "We got boiled ones, fruit drops, farthin' chews, mint humbugs, there's lollies, of course. They'se popular. There's strawberry, lemon, lime and orange."

Tom was annoyed at the long silence that followed and was just about to say something when he caught sight of Willie's face.

Willie swallowed hard. He'd never been asked to choose anything ever.

"A lolly please, miss," he said at last.

"What flavour?"

He frowned and panicked for a moment. "Strawberry," he answered huskily.

The old lady opened the jar and handed one to him. It was wrapped up in black-and-white striped paper and twisted like a unicorn's horn.

"Now what comic would you like, dear?"

Willie felt hopeless. What use would a comic be to him? He wouldn't be able to understand the words. He loved the colours, though, and the pictures looked so funny and exciting. He glanced up at Tom.

"I can't read, Mister Tom."

"I know that," he said shortly, "but I can."

from *Goodnight Mister Tom* by Michelle Magorian

UNIT·3 Writing to entertain

Text features:
comprehension,
old-fashioned
words
Reading/Writing
skills:
dialect and
standard English,
accent

1 The passage takes place

   in a shopping centre?   *in a market square?*
   in a village street?

2 The weather is

   fine and hot?   *cloudy and humid?*   *cold and wintry?*

3 Willie was stunned because

   he did not like sweets?   *he had never been allowed to
   choose sweets or comics?*   *he couldn't read?*

4 From the evidence in this passage,
   what sort of character is Mister Tom?

5 What do you learn about the
   character of Willie from the passage?

6 How do you think Willie felt about not being able to read?

   Accent is the way people pronounce words. It usually
   indicates where they come from.

7 How does the author indicate that the lady in the shop has a
   particular accent?

   Dialect is a variation in grammar or words in spoken
   English, depending on the speaker's origins.

8 Rewrite the following sentences of speech in standard
   English, as they might be written down, not spoken.
   EXAMPLE: We got a lot to do.
            We have got a lot to do.
   a You reckon you can keep up?
   b On market days that be filled with all kinds of stalls.
   c Hot, ent it?
   d You jest takes yer time.
   e They'se popular.

Glossary

accent
dialect

39

Slogans and proverbs

1 In the extract on page 38 the placard said 'Turn your wireless low. Someone might be on duty.' What did this mean?

2 Here are some other wartime **slogans**. Write a sentence to explain what each one could mean.

> **Proverbs** are sayings which have lasted for a long time and give some advice or insight into human life.

3 What do you think these proverbs mean?
   a A stitch in time saves nine.
   b Look after the pennies and
      the pounds look after themselves.
   c Waste not, want not.
   d Half a loaf is better than none.
   e A bird in the hand is worth two in the bush.

4 Why might these proverbs be particularly appropriate in wartime?

5 Match the two halves of the proverbs and write them out in full.

Too many cooks	before you leap.
The early bird	the mice do play.
Look	spoil the broth.
When the cat's away	a book by its cover.
Don't judge	catches the worm.

Remember
You can use a
dictionary of
proverbs to
help you
with this task.

Glossary
slogan

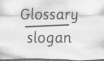

Another point of view

UNIT·3 **Writing to entertain**

Text level:
*comprehension,
summarising*
Reading skills:
*comprehension,
vocabulary*

1 Read the following extract from *War Horse* by
   Michael Morpurgo set in the First World War.

Chapter 5

In the few short weeks before I went off to war I was to be changed from a working farmhorse into a cavalry mount. It was no easy transformation, for I resented deeply the tight disciplines of the riding school and the hard hot hours out on manoeuvres on the Plain. Back at home with Albert I had revelled in the long rides along the lanes and over the fields; I had loved the aching days of ploughing and harrowing alongside Zoey, but that was because there had been a bond between us of trust and devotion.

But it was my rider that I disliked more than anything in my new life. Corporal Samuel Perkins was a hard, gritty little man, an ex-jockey whose only pleasure in life seemed to be the power he could exert over a horse. He was universally feared by all troopers and horses alike. Even the officers, I felt, went in trepidation of him; for he knew it seemed all there was to know about horses and had the experience of a lifetime behind him. And he rode hard and heavy-handed. With him the whip and the spurs were not just for show.

2 Write **definitions** of these words.
   a Cavalry means
   b Manoeuvres means
   c Harrowing means
   d Trepidation means

3 Who do you think Zoey was?

4 What role was the horse being prepared for?

5 **Summarise**, in note form, the passage above in four
   sentences or less. Remember to include the key issues:
   a who is involved
   b what the horse thinks about the changes.

6 Horses were used a great deal in the First World War,
   but not so much in the Second World War.
   a Why were less horses used in the Second World War?
   b What had taken the place of horses?
   c What disadvantages do horses have for fighting?

> **Remember**
> Some specialised words, like 'bit', have a number of definitions – choose the one that fits the passage.

> **Remember**
> Notes do not have to include full sentences.

> *Glossary*
> definition
> summary

UNIT·3 Writing to entertain

Text level:
*point of view,
anthropomorphism*
Reading skills:
vocabulary

Remember
Use a dictionary
and the Glossary
to help you
understand
difficult ideas.

A point of view

1 What does 'anthropomorphism' mean?

2 List two other books, films or poems that are anthropomorphic.

3 The other extracts in this unit have been told by an unknown narrator who revealed the characters' thoughts and feelings. Who tells the 'War Horse' story?

In the extract on page 41, the very first sentence tells the reader what happens. The rest of the **paragraph** describes the horse's thoughts and feelings.

4 Using the first paragraph of the extract on page 41 as a model, complete the paragraphs below.

In the term I have been in Mrs Flyte's class I have achieved remarkable progress in art...

The first few weeks after I was evacuated were an unhappy experience for me...

The outbreak of war totally changed our family's lives...

5 Imagine the paragraphs you have written were written by someone called Joe. Now rewrite one of the paragraphs in the third person.

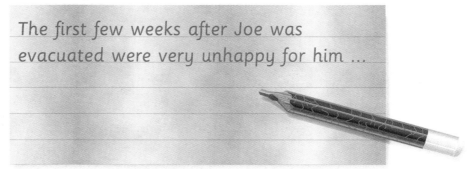

The first few weeks after Joe was
evacuated were very unhappy for him ...

Glossary
paragraph

Mnemonics

UNIT·3 Writing
to entertain

Word level
mnemonics
Sentence level
revising clauses

A **mnemonic** is a memory trick to help you remember
something, such as how to spell a word.

1 Explain how 'There is a rat in separate' helps you
to spell 'separate'.

2 Invent mnemonics of this type to help you spell:

   a friend (end)
   b piece (pie)
   c hear (ear).

3 What words do these mnemonics help you to spell?
   a Never Eat Cucumber, Eat Salad Sandwiches
     and Remain Young.
   b Wasps Always Sting.

4 Invent a mnemonic to help you spell:
   a because
   b people.

5 What words does this mnemonic help you to spell?

> **I before E except after C.**

Revising clauses

1 Add a clause to these clauses to make interesting sentences.
   a Even though it was raining
   b The war was terrible but
   c Sarah went to school although
   d because there was a war on.
   e until the war was over.
   f when the soldiers come home.

2 Put in commas or semi-colons to separate the clauses.

Even though the poor horse was tired he galloped bravely on.
The soldiers trudged wearily on despite the terrible weather.
The war was over there was peace at last.
She was an evacuee taken away from her normal home.

Writing a historical story

You are going to write a historical story set in the war. To do this you will need to discuss the period of history and look up information you might need to know.

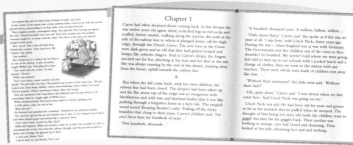

Brainstorm

1 You are going to write, as an adult, about your memories of being sent away from your parents to a strange place. This happened to thousands of children in the second world war. Even today many children are separated from their parents in wars and forced to become refugees.

2 Choose your character. Will you be a man or a woman? Write notes about your character as a child in wartime.
   - What does he/she look like?
   - What is his/her name?
   - What sort of clothes will he/she be wearing?
   - It is very important that you consider how you might feel if you had been sent away to the country without your parents. Remember, your character will be at least 60, but will talk about being a child in the war.

Plan

3 Make notes about the place in the country you have been sent to. Think about what the town or village would be like and how people might treat you. Choose a particular place to write about, such as a school, friend's house, play area or den.

4 Reread the extract from *Carrie's War* on pages 32 and 33. Notice how the author has
   - described the changes.
   - used detail about what she used to do to describe the place.
   - talked about another person in that place.
   - mentioned what other people said about the place.

5 Reread the extract from *Goodnight Mister Tom* on page 38. Notice how the author has used details about the place and time to create the atmosphere of the time.

6 To make your memories into a story you must think of an incident, happening or event which you are going to retell. Ideas could include an accident, a party, a school play, a sports day or anything else that would be memorable.

7 Now choose one of the introductory sentences below to begin your story and put in the name of your character.

_____ sometimes thought of the war, now that more than 50 years had passed since the end. He/she remembered the place where he/she was evacuated to _____.

When people talk about the horrors of the war,_____ remembered happy times. As an evacuee, life was not all bad.

Fifty years later _____ came back to the village. It had all changed but he/she remembered _____.

All through the war _____ was away from his/her family. Looking back to that time, he/she remembered one incident with clarity _____.

Draft

8 Now use your notes to write a plan of your story, taking care to use description to capture the sense of time passing and change.

9 Swap your draft with a friend. Discuss these questions.
- Is the story easy to understand?
- Are the characters easy to imagine?
- Have you managed to describe the place through what the character does?
- Does the story end well?

Discuss

10 Talk about these questions with your partner and mark any changes you want to make on the draft. Check any spellings you are not sure about.

11 Write out your story.

Publish

Writing to discuss

In this unit you will study how discussion documents are written. At the end of the unit you will plan, draft and write your own discussion piece on a controversial issue.

Tails fan anti-docking debate
by Peter Gruner

IF A SHEEPDOG wins the 109th Cruft's Show it will, for the first time, be able to celebrate by wagging its whole tail. Jezebel, an old English sheepdog, is believed to be the first of its breed to win a place in the semi-finals with its tail intact.

Campaigners against tail docking are celebrating the news as a small shift towards more natural looking dogs. The old English sheepdog and a Polish lowland sheepdog called Digby beat their docked rivals to qualify at the show at the NEC in Birmingham which opens on Thursday.

Owners and judges continue to defend the docking practice although it is regarded as unjustified mutilation by the Royal College of Veterinary Surgeons. A code of conduct issued by the RCVS seven

years ago bars vets from docking tails for cosmetic reasons but it can be justified for therapeutic reasons.

The campaigning editor of *Dogs Today*, Beverley Cuddy, described the two undocked dogs as a small but important 'breakthrough' for Cruft's.

"Until now, you would have had more chance of finding a cat than a

opening paragraphs indicate the area of disagreement

people in favour

UNIT·4 **Writing
to discuss**

Text features:
*issue,
arguments for,
arguments against*

- What is the purpose of this text?
- Are there arguments for and against?
- Why do you think the names of several organizations are given?
- What tense is most of this written in?

arguments against docking

causal links

boxer or an old English sheepdog with a tail, but times seem to be changing. Docking is cruel and crippling because the tail helps give the dog its sense of balance," she said.

Among the organizations opposed to docking are the RSPCA, which describes it as 'cruel', and the National Canine Defence League.

A quarter of the nation's 7.3 million dogs have had their tails removed, according to anti-docking campaigners who claim it is done for no other reason than because owners think it looks nice.

About 40 of the 170 species of dogs in Britain are docked – including boxers, cocker spaniels, Dobermans and Yorkshire terriers.

point backed by greater detail

In Germany an animal protection bill last year banned the docking of pet and show dogs' tails.

Raising the profile of dogs with tails is important to the Society for the Protection of Undocked Dogs which encouraged owners to show their undocked dogs. Caroline Kisko, spokeswoman for the Kennel Club, said the number of undocked dogs is increasing at Cruft's.

organizations/ individuals against

"We certainly don't have a view about the issue," she said. "Putting my own opinion aside, we have to remember that the claim that the practice is a cruel one has not been proved conclusively – and it is not against the law."

from *The Evening Standard* March 9, 1999

Comprehension and vocabulary

1 Look again at the article on pages 46 and 47.
  Answer these questions.

  a What two dogs (give their breed and their names) are
    through to the semi-final?

  b Why is their victory a 'breakthrough'?

  c How long ago did the Royal College of Veterinary
    Surgeons bar tail docking for cosmetic reasons?

  d Give two reasons owners give for docking tails.

  e Give two reasons campaigners give for docking
    being banned.

  f List three organizations that are against docking.

  g List two organizations that will tolerate docking.

  h How many docked dogs are there in Britain?

  i Which country recently banned the docking of dogs' tails?

  j The Kennel Club organizes the Cruft's show. Why do you
    think their spokesperson says they do not have a view
    about the issue?

Remember
You can use a
dictionary
to look up
word meanings.

2 Give a **definition** for the following words from the passage.

  a Celebrating means

  b Semi-finals means

  c Intact means

  d Unjustified means

  e Cosmetic means

  f Therapeutic means

3 Look at the **headline** to the article on pages 46 and 47.

4 Why do you think the verb 'fan' has been used?

5 Invent an alternative headline which includes a play
  on words. It can be about tail docking of any animal.

Tongues wag in docking debate

It's baaa baric

A tail tale

Expanding a point

UNIT·4 Writing
to discuss

Text features:
*elaborating on
arguments*
Word level:
*causal connectives,
proverbs*

In the article on pages 46 and 47 some facts are stated very
briefly. We can **extend arguments** by explaining the
significance of the fact.
EXAMPLE: In Germany an animal protection bill banned
the docking of tails. This shows that other countries have
recognized that it is unnecessary.

These **connectives** can help us expand a point into a more
persuasive **argument**.

this shows   therefore   we can see that
this means   in consequence   consequently
as a result   which makes   in view of which
thus   because

1 Use the connectives to expand each sentence into a
more extended argument.
   a Dogs cry out when their tails are docked.
   b Sheep with undocked tails are more likely to
   get dirt and disease gathering under their tails.
   c People continue to buy dogs with docked tails.
   d Tail docking is not illegal in the UK.

Proverbs

Proverbs are wise sayings which suggest ways of behaving.
Because dogs have been part of humans' lives for a long
time there are many proverbs which refer to dogs.
EXAMPLE: Don't keep a dog and bark yourself.
This means don't do a job someone else can do for you.

2 What do these proverbs mean?
   a Every dog will have its day.
   b You cannot run with the hare
   and hunt with the hounds.

3 Make up your own dog proverb.

Glossary
connective
argument

49

UNIT·4 Writing to discuss

Text features:
*arguments for
and against*
Word level:
*persuasive
language*

Animal testing: For and against

Using animals for laboratory testing is a topic people disagree about.

1 Sort out these **arguments** into groups for and against.

Animals are different from humans and so any evidence from animal testing cannot apply to humans.

Most scientists care a great deal about the animals they use and animal research is strictly controlled by law.

Animals are used for frivolous experiments such as testing cosmetics.

Animal research is morally wrong.

It would be morally wrong to let people be ill or in pain if animal testing can provide new cures.

There are great similarities between animal and human reactions to medicines.

We can use computers or test-tube experiments instead of animals.

Computers and test-tube experiments are used as much as possible but we also need to use animals before testing on humans.

Animal research is essential for the development of new medicines for serious illnesses.

Animals are cruelly treated in laboratories.

2 The words we choose can influence people. 'Frivolous', 'wrong' and 'cruelly' have all been chosen to make animal testing sound horrible. Find three words or phrases that those in favour of testing have chosen to make their case sound right.

3 What is the main difference between the two **viewpoints**? Complete this sentence.

Some people believe that animals ...whilst others believe ....

4 Use the arguments above to write two paragraphs. Add any further ideas you have.

Those people who think animals should not be used for experiments argue that ...
The people who support animal experimentation for the development of medicines claim ...

5 What do you think? Write a sentence giving your views.

I think that ...

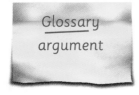

Glossary
argument

Facts and opinions

When reading and writing discussions it is important to be able to sort out facts from opinions. It is also important to recognize phrases and words which are included to influence our thinking.

1 Read this and find three facts and two opinions.

In 1986 the government created the Animals (Scientific Procedures) Act. The Act controls all aspects of the use of animals in research. It aims to balance any likely adverse effects on animals against the benefits to humans and animals likely to result from any proposed research. It is thought that this law is the most comprehensive of its kind in the world. To carry out animal experiments each research project must be granted a licence by the Secretary of State. This is a good idea. The application must describe fully the research programme and list the species and numbers of animals to be used.

People can try to make their **arguments** and opinions sound stronger by adding **persuasive phrases** and **words**.

EXAMPLES: Of course this is a good idea.
Everybody thinks this is a good idea.

2 Add some persuasive phrases to these sentences.

we all agree *unquestionably* **without doubt**
it is undeniable **definitely**

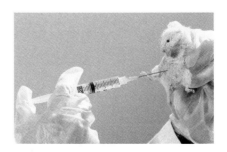

  a All scientists look after animals carefully.
  b Animal testing is wrong.
  c People are more important than animals.
  d Some experiments are justifiable but not the testing of cosmetics.

3 Pictures can strengthen arguments. Which of these pictures would you choose if you supported or disagreed with animal experiments?

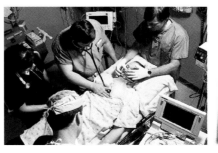

Glossary
argument

51

The Zoo Debate

We are now going to look at another example of discussion writing. This author uses humour to express the ideas.

illustrations and headings to appeal to a particular age group

Zoos: Conservation or Cruelty?

Taking a trip to the zoo may be fun for you, but how much do the animals enjoy it? Being a zoo animal is a 24-hour job – unlike you, the animals can't go home at the end of the day to roam in their natural habitat. On the other hand, zoos can teach us a great deal about animals, which in turn may help us to protect endangered species. So what are the pros and cons in the great zoo debate?

Too Close for Comfort
Many animals are not used to being close to humans and may find it disturbing. (If you think your family are strange, imagine how they must seem to the average polar bear!)

arguments against

Lonely Lions
Some animals need to get together with their own kind. In zoos, naturally sociable animals are sometimes left without family or friends and feel isolated and confused.

persuasive language

Bored Bears go Barmy
Because they can't lead natural lives, zoo animals run the risk of developing abnormal behaviour patterns. Repetitive pacing, rocking from side to side and biting the bars are signs that animals may be suffering from 'zoochosis' (not a new pop group, but a brainy scientific term to describe this sad behaviour).

arguments for

It's Not all Boos to Zoos
The good news is that zoos can play a very valuable role in research and conservation. Some animals would actually be extinct without their help. The Hawaiian goose, Pere David's deer and the Golden Lion tamarin may all have disappeared without the help of zoo breeding programmes.

words/ phrases signalling change of stance

Freeing all the animals in every zoo in Britain probably won't help them all that much. On the other hand zoos do vary enormously in the quality of the care and conditions that they give to the animals. Some provide much better homes than others. Good zoos make sure that monkeys have room to swing around and the penguins space to swim.

What do your friends and teachers think about zoos?
Why not ask your teacher to organize a class debate?

from *Roar! Animal Rights Handbook for Kids* by Peter Hoggarth

Text features:
*issue, arguments
for, arguments
against*
Reading skills:
comprehension
Word level:
definitions

1 Read the passage carefully then answer these questions.
  a Give two reasons in favour of zoos.
  b Give two reasons against zoos.
  c What might happen to sociable animals who are left alone?
  d What sort of abnormal behaviour patterns might animals develop in zoos?
  e Name two species that have been helped by zoo breeding programmes.
  f Give two examples of good living conditions in zoos.
  g Which side of the argument do you find most persuasive? Why?

2 Give a **definition** for the following words from the passage.
  a Habitat means
  b Endangered means
  c Bored means
  d Sociable means
  e Abnormal means
  f Conservation means

> **Remember**
> You can use a dictionary to look up word meanings.

3 Write out an example of an alliterative heading from page 52.

4 Why do you think the author has used alliteration?

5 What else has the author used to appeal to his readers?

> Glossary
> definition

Switching arguments

When we are looking at differing points of view it is helpful to the reader if we signal when we are going to change sides. Certain **connective** words and phrases can help us do this.

EXAMPLE: Animals are well looked after in zoos *but* they may be bored.

1 Here are some contrastive connectives.

whereas   but   on the other hand   however

a counter argument   against that   instead

in contrast   although   alternatively

2 Sort out these statements into contrasting pairs.

People can get close to animals in zoos.

It is convenient to come to school by car.

Animals bred in zoos are rarely released into the wild.

In the summer the sun is too hot.

Wild animals may be disturbed by the presence of people.

The heat of the sun can be relaxing.

People making short car journeys cause congestion

Endangered animals can breed in zoos.

3 Use the connectives given above to link the pairs of statements.

4 Find two examples of contrastive connectives being used in the passage on Tail Docking on pages 46 and 47.

5 Find an example in the passage on Zoos on page 52.

Conditional sentences

Conditional sentences contain a **subordinate clause** beginning with **if**, **when** or **unless**. They express generalizations, predictions or possibilities – things that will, should, might or could happen.

1 Add a **main clause** to these subordinate clauses to make conditional sentences.
   a When it rains ▢ .
   b Unless she gets here soon ▢ .
   c If you like animals ▢ .
   d Unless we stop them ▢ .
   e When you hear the bell ▢ .
   f If you don't study hard ▢ .

Some verbs are important for expressing conditional happenings. These are **modal verbs** and they are usually used with other verbs, not on their own.
The modal verbs are:

**must   can   may   will   shall
could   might   would   should**

2 Use one of the modal verbs to complete these conditional sentences.
   a If you support animal rights you ▢ write to your MP.
   b When you buy eggs you ▢ look for free range ones.
   c Unless dogs are well exercised they ▢ get fat.
   d Dogs ▢ not have their tails docked unless there is good reason.
   e When scientists conduct experiments they ▢ use computers instead of animals.
   f Unless we ban whale hunting, certain whales ▢ become extinct.

3 Compare your sentences with a partner's. Have you both used the same modal verbs? If not, does it make any difference to the meaning of the sentence?

Glossary
subordinate clause
main clause

55

Letter writing

You can get information on the pros and cons of animal issues by writing to animal organizations.

1 Look at this letter.

```
bidmouth wildlife zoo            seaton rise school
bidmouth                         bidmouth
bn6 4rt                          bn3 4rt
                                 7th march 1999

dear mr smith

my class is undertaking some research in order to
write a discussion paper about whether animals should
be kept in zoos

we have heard about your conservation programme and
we would like to ask you for some more details about
it how many endangered animals have been born since
you began the programme and have any been
successfully returned to the wild we would also like
to ask where you buy your animals from and whether
you know if they have been taken from the wild if you
have any information leaflets about your programme we
would be grateful if you could send us a copy

this information will help us get an accurate picture
of how your zoo works and will help us write a
balanced discussion paper

thank you for your help.

yours sincerely
ben wright
(on behalf of class 6)
```

2 Ben had a problem with the computer when he was typing this letter and has missed out all capital letters and punctuation marks. Correct the mistakes, using the copy of the letter that your teacher will give you.

3 Why has Ben used a formal style and not a chatty style of writing?

4 At the end of this unit you are going to write a discussion paper on fox hunting. Use Ben's letter as a model to write your own letter to one of these organizations asking for information.

```
Countryside Alliance
The Old Town Hall
367 Kennington Road
London
SE11 4PT
```

```
The League Against Cruel Sports
83-87 Union Street
London
SE1 1SG
```

Inflated language

UNIT·4 Writing
to discuss

Word level:
inflated language
Grammar:
passive voice

Official notices, letters and documents often use more formal language than spoken language. It may include:

- long words instead of simple words
  – 'suspended'
- the use of set phrases
  – 'due to circumstances'
- flattery and/or apology
  – 'we regret to announce'
- upgrading of job titles
  – 'Animal Comfort Operative'
- use of the passive voice –
  'have been suspended'.

Over-use of these can sound pompous and inflated. Careful use can make writing seem more authoritative.

We regret to announce that due to circumstances beyond our control (incapacity of Animal Comfort Operative), admissions to the reptile house have been suspended until further notice.

Sorry. It's closed. The keeper's phoned in sick.

1 Find one example of each of these in the reply Ben received to his letter to the Zoo.

Ben Wright
Seaton Rise School
Bidmouth
BN3 4RT

 Bidmouth Wildlife
Bidmouth
BN6 4RT

12th March 1999

Dear Ben,

We are delighted that we had the opportunity to welcome you and your colleagues to our zoo. We trust you found your visit interesting and everything to your satisfaction. Our Animal Comfort Operatives are of the highest calibre and our animal inmate enclosures are maintained to the highest standards of hygiene and comfort.

Thank you for your query regarding our renowned Animal Breeding Programme. Leaflets are enclosed for your information.

If we can be of any further assistance to you and your educational establishment, please do not hesitate to contact me or a member of my customer care team.

Assuring you of our best attention at all times.
Yours sincerely,

Mr P Smith
(Manager, Customer Care Directorate)

2 Write a simplified version of Mr Smith's letter.

Writing a discussion paper

You have looked at different controversial issues in this unit. Now you are going to write your own discussion paper looking at the arguments for and against another animal issue, fox hunting.

Discuss

1   Look at the discussions you have studied in this unit.

2   In pairs, discuss each of these ideas in favour of hunting. Record your ideas on the grid your teacher will give you.

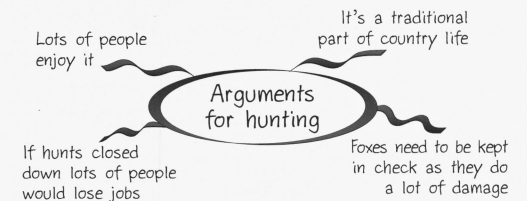

Lots of people enjoy it

It's a traditional part of country life

Arguments for hunting

If hunts closed down lots of people would lose jobs

Foxes need to be kept in check as they do a lot of damage

3   In different pairs, discuss each of these ideas against hunting. Record your ideas on the grid your teacher will give you.

Plan

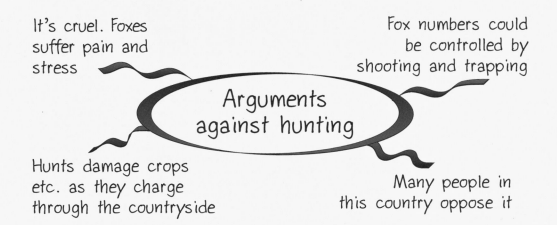

It's cruel. Foxes suffer pain and stress

Fox numbers could be controlled by shooting and trapping

Arguments against hunting

Hunts damage crops etc. as they charge through the countryside

Many people in this country oppose it

4 If you have access to any books, leaflets, or the Internet, find evidence to add to your points (for example, how many people belong to hunting organizations, how many people belong to anti-hunting organizations).

5 Write an opening sentence stating what the disagreement is. Then add a couple of sentences outlining the key arguments on each side.

6 Write a paragraph supporting hunting and a paragraph against hunting. Use your notes to help you. Set out your points and back them up with evidence.

7 Write a conclusion summing up what you have said and giving your opinion if you wish.

8 Share your draft with a friend.

Draft

Revise

Publish

- Has your choice of words suggested where your sympathy lies?
- Are the arguments clear?
- Are they backed up with any evidence or is it just opinion?
- Have you concluded by summarizing the arguments and stating your view?

9 Make any alterations you decide are needed. Check spelling, punctuation and paragraphing.

10 Complete a final version of your discussion paper.

Writing to explain

In this unit you will study how explanations are written.
Explanations usually answer the questions 'how?', 'what is?'
and 'why?'. At the end of the unit you will plan, draft and
write your own explanation.

sequence of events explained

⚙ HOW THINGS WORK

Washing machine

opening summary statement

A modern washing machine relies on several regulatory mechanisms in its operation. At the start of the cycle, water pours in through an electrically controlled inlet valve. Once the water reaches a certain level in the drum this is detected by a sensor that closes the inlet valve.

sentence in passive voice

The pressure of the water in the inlet pipe helps to shut the valve firmly. The water is then heated by the machine's heater element. Once the pre-set temperature is reached, a thermostat switches off the electricity supply to the heater. A load of washing and water is very heavy, so the drum is stabilized by weights and suspended by heavy-duty springs.

action and results

causal connective

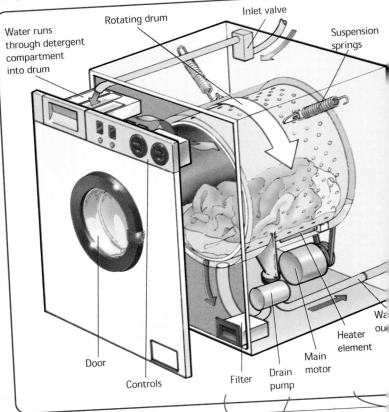

Water runs through detergent compartment into drum

Rotating drum

Inlet valve

Suspension springs

Door

Controls

Filter

Drain pump

Main motor

Heater element

Wa ou

technical language

UNIT·5 Writing to explain

Text features:
statement, details,
technical
vocabulary,
diagram

- What is the purpose of this text?
- Why is technical language needed?
- Why is a diagram needed?
- Why is an authoritative tone used?
- Why is the present tense used?

phenomena to be explained

Tumble drier

In most tumble driers the electric motor is programmed to turn the drum one way and then go into reverse and spin it the other way. This helps to shake and separate the contents. It prevents them from clumping together and leaving a still damp patch in the middle which the drying air cannot reach. Hot air is drawn through the unit by a blower fan. As it passes through the load, the air picks up dust and fibres; these are

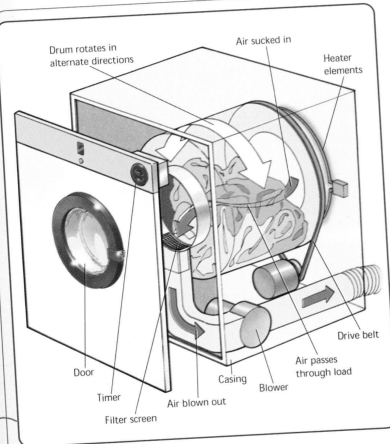

Drum rotates in alternate directions

Air sucked in

Heater elements

Door

Timer

Filter screen

Air blown out

Casing

Blower

Air passes through load

Drive belt

trapped by the filter screen. In order to heat such great volumes of air, tumble driers use lots of electricity. They have one of the highest running costs of all household machines.

diagram to clarify and add more detail

from *The Kingfisher Book of How Things Work* by Steve Parker

Comprehension and vocabulary

1 Look again at explanations on pages 60 and 61. Answer these questions.
   a What happens at the start of a washing-machine cycle?
   b How does the detergent get into the drum?
   c Why are there suspension springs inside the washing-machine case?
   d What would happen to wet washing if it stayed clumped together?
   e What happens to dust and fibres in tumble driers?
   f Why are tumble driers expensive to run?
   g Why do you think the tumble drier does not need weights and springs to stabilize it?

2 Give a **definition** for the following words from the passage.
   a Regulatory means
   b Rotating means
   c Stabilized means
   d Reverse means
   e Filter means
   f Pre-set means

Remember
You can use a dictionary to look up word meanings.

3 Kitchens are full of machines to help make domestic jobs easier. Can you create an alphabetical list of electrical machines you might find in a kitchen?

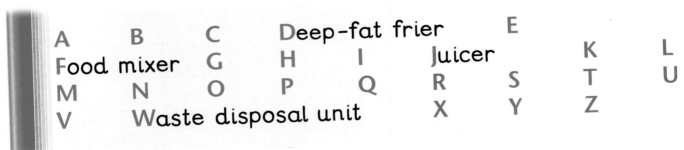

A   B   C   Deep-fat frier   E
Food mixer   G   H   I   Juicer   K   L
M   N   O   P   Q   R   S   T   U
V   Waste disposal unit   X   Y   Z

Glossary
definition

Joining sentences: cause and effect

Explanations often include a description of action followed by the effect of that action.

EXAMPLE: Once the pre-set temperature is reached, a thermostat switches off the electricity supply. We could join these two clauses together with a causal connective.

EXAMPLE: Once the pre-set temperature is reached *this causes* a thermostat to switch off the electricity supply.

1   Here are some more causal connectives to link actions and effects.

because   this causes   so   consequently
as a result   this makes   and so   as

2   Here are some actions and their effects (results). Use a causal connective to make each pair into one sentence.

Remember
Your linking words can come at the beginning or in the middle of the sentence.

Action	Effect
The water reaches a certain level.	The inlet valve closes.
The drier drum turns one way and then the other.	The contents are shaken and separated.
Hot air passes through the load.	Air picks up dust and fibres.
The machine needs a lot of hot air.	It uses a great deal of electricity.
A washing machine load is heavy.	The drum has to be weighed down to stabilize it.
Water runs through the detergent compartment.	Detergent is taken into the drum.

3   Finish these sentences by adding an effect (result) to the action.
   a   I forgot to do my homework   .
   b   The wind was very strong   .
   c   I had spent all my pocket money by Monday   .
   d   The dustbin was overflowing   .

Creating new words

As new machines are invented they are often named after the job they do or what makes them work.

EXAMPLE: **dishwasher, tumble drier, microwave oven**

1 Here are some ideas for new machines. Choose one. Draw what you think it might look like and invent a new name for it. A machine that will:

a change your thoughts into writing on a computer screen.

b tidy your bedroom.

c unpack the supermarket shopping for you.

2 Write a few sentences explaining how your machine works.

3 Here are some new words from *The Oxford Dictionary of New Words*.

Ofsted   sleeping policeman   Euro   rollover   superhighway   Britpop

4 Write your own **definition** for three of these words.

Sometimes new words are old words used in a new way.

EXAMPLE: **Wicked**   old meaning:bad/evil

new meaning:great/trendy

5 Make a chart with other examples you can think of. Compare your chart with a friend's.

Word	Old meaning	New meaning
anorak	a jacket	a person who does boring things

Mixed texts

Sometimes a written text may have more than one purpose.

How You can Reduce Your Waste

WISE UP TO WASTE

Try using the following tips to reduce your waste

- Think before you buy. Choose products with less packaging.
- Take a reusable bag when you go shopping. Ask your local supermarket if they supply reusable bags or boxes.
- Compost your kitchen and garden waste. Not only will you reduce your waste but you will also produce a soil conditioner for your garden. Contact your District Council for compost bin details.
- Buy in bulk to reduce packaging and save money.
- Avoid using disposable items like paper plates or plastic cups.
- Buy low energy light bulbs and save both energy and money.
- If you use batteries, why not use rechargeable ones?

- Have your shoes and household items repaired.
- Donate your unwanted clothes, shoes and bric-a-brac to your local charity shop.
- Avoid unwanted circulars and free papers by putting a sticker on your letter box (available from Devon County Council).
- Avoid junk mail by writing to:
  Mailing Preference Service
  Freepost 22
  London WIE 7EZ
  asking them to remove you from mailing lists.
- Support refillable bottle systems.
  Recycle what you can.
  Find out where your nearest Recycling Centre is and use it.
  Ask your District Council where your nearest recycling banks are.

This leaflet gives ideas about how to reduce waste. The ideas are given as **instructions** and the **explanation** is often implied rather than stated.

EXAMPLE: 'Choose products with less packaging' (written) implies – because you will have less packaging to throw away.

1 Choose three tips from the leaflet. Add a reason for the tip (as panel above) to make the explanation clearer.

2 How could you reduce waste in your classroom? List some ideas giving reasons so that the explanations are clear.

> *In order to save paper use scrap paper, not new paper, for rough work.*

3 Create a small leaflet that explains how to reduce waste in your classroom. It should include tips and reasons, your icon and your **slogan**.

Glossary
slogan

Anagrams and palindromes

There are many different ways of playing with words in the English language.

> An **anagram** is when the letters of a word or phrase are jumbled up to make a new word or phrase.
> EXAMPLES: the Morse code = here come dots
> world cup team = talcum powder

1 Try unscrambling these anagrams. They all make the name of a famous person or group. The first one is done for you.
  a I am a weakish speller = William Shakespeare
  b Crisis! Get help = (a girl pop group)
  c Aim and saved = (England goalkeeper)
  d Lean and solemn = (former President of South Africa)
  e Ten elite brains = (scientist, invented the theory
        of relativity)

2 Try making an anagram for a kitchen machine, e.g. a washing machine.

> **Palindromes** are words or sentences that say the same when read backwards or forwards.
> EXAMPLES: dad   oxo
>   A man, a plan, a canal, Panama!

3 Make a list of all the palindromic words you can think of.

4 It is very difficult to create a sentence palindrome.
  Try, but don't worry if you only manage a word or two.

Pangrams and lipograms

Pangrams are sentences that contain all the letters
of the alphabet.
EXAMPLE: The quick brown fox jumped over the lazy dog.

1 Try writing a pangram. Use a dictionary to help you.

2 Swap with a partner and check that they
have used all the letters of the alphabet.

Extra Postage will be charged for heavy boxes to
be moved quickly to zones J and M. (66 letters)

3 Count how many letters you took to create your sentence.
Who managed it in the least number of letters?

4 Now try to write a pangram that contains the words
'washing machine' or 'tumble drier.'

A lipogram is a sentence which does not
use a particular given letter, such as 'e'.
EXAMPLE: All good boys should
drink six cups of liquid a day.

> **DID YOU KNOW?**
> Georges Perec wrote a
> novel without using the
> letter 'e'.

5 Ask a partner to tell you which letter you cannot use, then
write the longest sentence you can without using the letter.

6 Swap with your partner and ask them to check that you have
not used the letter.

7 Count how many letters you took to create your sentence.
Who managed the longest sentence?

8 Write a lipogram sentence about a washing machine.
Do not use the letter 'o'.

Another explanation

The explanation at the beginning of the unit answered the question 'how'? Here is another explanation answering the questions 'what is a ...?' and 'why'.

specialist vocabulary

phenomenon to be explained given in the headings

diagram to clarify and add detail

causal links

summary answer explaining what it is

further details given

Reflex actions

A reflex action is an action your body makes automatically. They happen because your brain sometimes quickly flashes a message to your nerves telling them to do something. You cannot stop a reflex action from happening.

Sneezing

You sneeze in order to clear quickly something that is tickling your nose. Sneezing is a reflex action. You breathe in deeply and then air is blown out of your nose and mouth with great force.

Sneezing helps spread disease because tiny drops of mucus containing bacteria and viruses fly out with the air. This is why you should sneeze into a handkerchief.

 When you sneeze, the air travels at more than 160 kilometres per hour.

Yawning

Yawning is a reflex action that makes you open your mouth wide, breathe in, and then breathe out slowly. You do this when you do not have as much oxygen as you need. This happens when you are tired, or bored, or when you are in a stuffy room and need fresh air. Yawning helps you to take in extra oxygen.

Vomiting

You vomit when food rushes up from your stomach and out through your mouth. It is a reflex action caused by the muscles in your abdomen tightening up and forcing the contents of your stomach back up. Vomiting may be caused by eating too much or by food poisoning. Some people also vomit from travel sickness. Travel sickness happens because the movement of the vehicle disturbs the balance organ in each ear.

from *The Oxford Children's A–Z of the Human Body* by Bridget and Neil Ardley

Text features:
*summary,
explanation,
details, cause
and effect*
Word level:
*definitions,
causal
conjunctions*

1 Look carefully at the passage and diagram.
Answer these questions.
  a Why can you not stop a reflex action from happening?
  b What is spread by sneezing?
  c Name two situations that might cause yawning?
  d What is the effect of yawning?
  e How does travelling cause travel sickness?

2 Give a definition for the following words from the passage.
  a Automatically means
  b Tickling means
  c Stuffy means
  d Contents means
  e Disturbs means

3 Here are some actions (causes) and their effects (results).
Use the information in the passage to complete the chart.

Cause	Action	Effect
		You should use a handkerchief.
You do not have enough oxygen.	Yawn	
You are bored.		
The muscles in your abdomen tighten up.		
Vehicles move.		

UNIT·5 Writing
to explain

Grammar:
*compound
sentences,
complex sentences,
main and
subordinate
clauses*
Word level:
causal connectives

Compound and complex sentences

A **compound sentence** is made up of two or more **main clauses**.
EXAMPLES: Yawning takes in extra oxygen (main clause) so yawning helps you to stay awake (main clause).
A **complex sentence** is made up of a **main clause** and one or more **subordinate clauses** or phrases.
EXAMPLES: By taking in extra oxygen (subordinate phrase), yawning helps you stay awake (main clause).

Remember
A clause always contains a verb.

1 Decide whether these are complex or compound sentences.
   a When you sneeze you breathe in deeply and then air is blown out.
   b Mucus, which contains bacteria and viruses, is spread by sneezing.
   c You cannot stop a reflex action because it happens automatically.
   d Coughing loudly, she had to leave the concert.
   e He was away from school as he had a terrible cold.

Adding clauses or phrases can make simple sentences more interesting. In explanations the clauses or phrases are often linked with **causal connectives** such as **because**, **by**, **so**, **therefore**, **this means that**.
EXAMPLES: Coughing spreads disease.
                     By scattering germs around, coughing spreads disease.

Remember
The rules for punctuating complex sentences are given on p11.

2 Add a further main clause or subordinate clause or phrase to these sentences. Use a causal connective.
   a You have a high temperature.
   b She took a travel sickness pill.
   c They tried hard not to yawn.
   d I feel sick.
   e It is hygienic to cover your mouth when you cough.
   f Lack of oxygen makes you sleepy.

Glossary
main clause
subordinate
clause

3 Write 'complex' or 'compound' next to each of the new sentences you have created.

Verb tenses

Most reports are written in the present tense.

> **Verbs tenses** tell us whether something
> is happening now, has already happened
> or will happen in the future.
> EXAMPLES:
> you yawn, you are yawning (present)
> you yawned, you have yawned (past)
> you will yawn (future)

1   Find all the present tense verbs (or verb + auxiliary verb)
    in the report below.

> **Remember**
> A verb may
> have an auxiliary
> verb with it.
> This also indicates
> the tense.

MINISTRY OF HEALTH SAYS –
COUGHS AND SNEEZES SPREAD DISEASES –

trap the germs in your handkerchief

HELP TO KEEP THE NATION FIGHTING FIT

You sneeze in order to clear quickly something
that is tickling your nose. Sneezing is a reflex
action. You breathe in deeply and then air is
blown out of your nose and mouth with great
force. Sneezing helps spread disease because
tiny drops of mucus containing bacteria and
viruses fly out with the air. This is why you
should sneeze into a handkerchief.

2   Change this passage from the past tense to the future tense.
    You may have to change more than the verbs.

Yesterday I went to visit my uncle. As usual, he told
me lots of jokes and I laughed and laughed and
laughed. I started to hiccup. It got worse and worse.
My family suggested lots of cures. They told me to
hold my breath. That did not work. They dropped a
cold object down my back. That did not work. They
crept up behind me and shouted to scare me. That
did not work. They told me to sip a glass of water.
That did not work. Finally it stopped…but then my
uncle started telling jokes again.

3   Identify two irregular past tense verbs in the passage.

4   Write a three-sentence, present tense account of what you
    are doing right now.

Writing an explanation

You have looked at different types of explanations in this unit.
Now you are going to write your own explanation of another
reflex action.

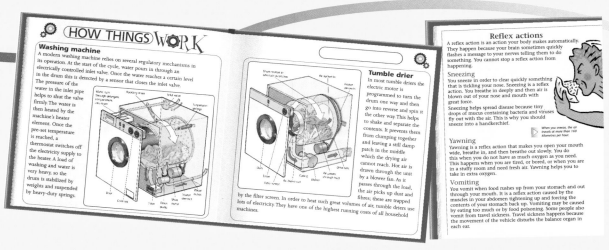

1 Look at the passages you have studied in this unit.

2 With a partner, talk about the characteristics of an
explanation. The annotations on pages 60, 61 and 68
will help you.

3 Now you are going to think about what happens when you
have a reflex action caused by someone coming up behind
you, or making a noise, when you are not expecting it.

4 List all the things your body does.

> body, arms, legs –
> heart –
> sound –
> breathing –

Plan

5 Try to decide why each of these reactions happens.
Talk about it with others if you are not sure.
Add the reasons to your list.

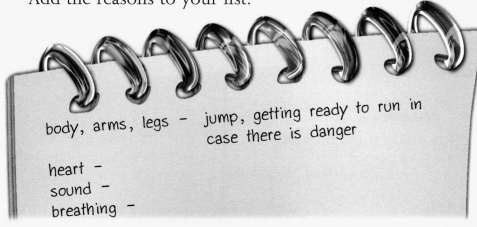

> body, arms, legs – jump, getting ready to run in
> case there is danger
>
> heart –
> sound –
> breathing –

6 Turn your list into sentences using causal connectives.

> You breathe more rapidly in order to take in more oxygen. This means you are very awake and are ready to move quickly if you have to escape.

7 Decide on a heading for your explanation.

> Why do we jump at sudden noises?

8 Answer your question with a general answer by completing these sentences.

> Jumping at unexpected movement or noises is a reflex...
>
> Reflex actions are...

9 Now go on to complete a first draft of your explanation. You can add details by using the causal sentences you have created in step 6.

> When we have this kind of reflex action several things happen...

Draft

Discuss

Publish

10 Discuss your draft with a friend and revise it if necessary.

- Is it clear?
- Does it give reasons for the actions?
- Does anything need further explanation?

11 Edit your spelling and punctuation.

12 Complete a final version of your explanation.

Glossary

accent
The way a person pronounces what they say. Speakers used different accents depending on their origins and the situation in which they are speaking. Not to be confused with **dialect**.

active voice
A sentence or phrase in which the subject is the person or thing doing or being the verb. EXAMPLE: The man **ate** the cake.
A passive sentence or phrase is one in which the subject is being acted on by the verb. EXAMPLE: The cake **was eaten** by the man.
Passive forms occur in formal writing and scientific reports.

adjective
A word that goes with a noun and tells us about it. EXAMPLE: a **blue** balloon. A comparative adjective can be used to compare nouns.
EXAMPLE: The boy was **bigger** than his friend. A superlative adjective can be used to compare something with all the others.
EXAMPLE: The boy was the **biggest** in the class. A possessive adjective describes who the noun belongs to: *mine, his, her, your, their*.

adverb
A word that tells us about a verb. Some adverbs have the suffix -ly.
EXAMPLE: happily. Common types of adverbs include adverbs of:

Degree	adverbs which modify another adverb: more, very
Manner	softly, happily
Time	soon, now
Place	here, there

agent
In a sentence the agent is the person or thing performing or being the verb. EXAMPLE: The boy pushed Bob. The *boy* is the agent.
In a passive sentence the agent may be indicated using 'by'.
EXAMPLE: Bob was pushed *by the boy*.
In a passive sentence the agent may be left out to make the writing less personal. EXAMPLE: Bob was pushed.

agreement
In sentences some words or phrases are linked in meaning.
This means they *agree* in terms of:

Tense	*yesterday* we *went* out
Number	the *dogs* ate *their* dinner
Gender	the *girl* picked up *her* coat
Person	I want *my* mum!

apostrophe
An apostrophe is a mark used to show that a letter has been left out.
EXAMPLE: *he is* can be written as *he's*
Apostrophes are also used to show ownership. EXAMPLES: the cat's bowl (one cat), the cats' bowls (more than one cat).

argument
A written argument makes a point and gives evidence to support it.

autobiography
A life story of a person written by that person.

auxiliary verb
See **verb**. Usually the verbs to be, to have or to do.

biography
A life story of a person written by another author.

bracket
A punctuation mark used to indicate **parenthesis**.

bullet point
A punctuation mark used to emphasise items in a list.

cast list
A list of characters in a play.

character	A character is an individual in a story, play or poem. The things characters do and say tell us what they are like.
chronological order	Chronological order is the order in which events happen. Chronological writing is written in time order. EXAMPLE: an account of a day that starts in the morning and goes through to the evening.
clause (main and subordinate)	A distinct part of a sentence including a verb. A main clause makes sense on its own. A subordinate clause adds detail to the main clause but does not make sense on its own. EXAMPLE: Although it was foggy, I went out. 　　　　(subordinate clause)　　(main clause)
colon	A punctuation mark used to introduce a list. It can also be used to introduce a quotation, or a second clause which expands the first.
comma	A punctuation mark used to break up sentences so that they are easier to understand. Commas are used to separate items in a list that is part of a sentence. EXAMPLE: I bought eggs, fish and some chocolate. Commas are also used to separate clauses. EXAMPLE: Although she is old, the cat is beautiful. Commas can be used for parenthesis (embedding extra information in a sentence). EXAMPLE: The cat, which was very old, was sitting on the mat.
command	A type of sentence that tells someone what to do. Uses imperative verbs.
common gender words	A word which can refer to men, women or both. EXAMPLE: passenger, doctor
complex sentence	See sentence
compound word	A word made from two other words. EXAMPLE: footpath
conjunction	A word used to join sentences or parts of sentences. EXAMPLES: and, but, then, because
connective	A word or group of words, which links sentences or parts of sentences. EXAMPLES: and, then, but, even, so
dash	A punctuation mark used in a number of ways. For instance, instead of brackets or commas for parenthesis. In informal writing or notes a dash is used to replace other punctuation.
definition	A statement giving the meaning of a word or phrase.
description	Words which enable the reader/listener to form an idea of an object, event or feeling.
dialect	Variations in grammar and vocabulary of spoken or written English which reflect the speaker's origins or situation.
dialogue	Speech between two or more people.
direct speech	Speech written exactly as it is said. In books this is usually in speech marks. In a playscript direct speech is not placed in speech marks.
event	Something which happens.
exclamation	A type of sentence that expresses feeling. Exclamations end with an exclamation mark. EXAMPLE: Help me, please!
exclamation mark	A punctuation mark used at the end of a sentence to indicate strong feelings. EXAMPLE: Help!

first person	The first person pronoun is **I**. In writing it is used when the writer is writing about him or herself.
formal language/ informal language	Formal language is the speech and writing we use for people we do not know well. EXAMPLE: How do you do? Informal language is the language we use to people we know well. EXAMPLE: Hi!
full stop	A mark used to end a sentence when the sentence is not a question or exclamation. EXAMPLE: The cat sat on the mat.
headline	A prominent heading.
imperative	An imperative word commands or tells the reader or listener to do something. EXAMPLE: Run over there.
metaphor	A metaphor is when the writer writes about something as if it were something else. EXAMPLES: Food for thought. Rise and shine.
narrator	The person whose voice is heard in a novel or story. The narrator can be one of the characters speaking (first person) or someone speaking about the characters (third person). In a play the narrator may speak about what is happening to the characters on stage.
noun	A word that names a person, feeling or thing.
paragraph	A section of a piece of writing which marks a change of focus, time, place or speaker in the writing. A paragraph begins a new line.
parenthesis	Embedding extra information in a sentence using commas, dashes or brackets. EXAMPLES: The cat, which was very old, was sitting on the mat. The cat - which was very old - was sitting on the mat. The cat (which was very old) was sitting on the mat.
passive	See **active voice**
phrase	Two or more words which act as a unit.
playscript	A playscript displays dialogue clearly so that actors can read it. Stage directions tell actors how to behave.
plural	More than one.
preposition	A word telling us about the place of nouns or pronouns. EXAMPLES: on, under, in
present tense/ past tense	See **tense**.
pronoun	A word used instead of a noun or noun phrase to avoid repetition in a sentence. EXAMPLE: **The cat** was old but **she** was sprightly. Personal pronouns: I, me, we, us, you, they, them Possessive pronouns: my, your, their, his, hers
proper noun	A words that names a particular person, thing or feeling. Proper nouns begin with a capital letter. EXAMPLES: Christmas, London, Jamilla
question	A sentence which needs a response. It ends with a question mark. EXAMPLE: What is your name?
question mark	The punctuation mark at the end of a sentence.
recount	A text which retells events for entertainment and/or information. Written or told in the past tense.

reported speech	A report of what has been said, not in the exact words of the speaker.
rhyme	Words that sound the same at the end when spoken, but may not be spelt the same. EXAMPLES: cat/bat; pain/mane
rhythm	The pattern of sounds within a piece of writing. The 'beats' in a line of poetry.
semi-colon	A punctuation mark which separates phrases or clauses in a sentence. It is used to separate items in a list (when the item is more than one word). A semi-colon also acts as a connective between two clauses of equal weight in a sentence. EXAMPLES: It was a dark night; the moon hid behind a cloud.
sentence	A unit of written language which makes sense on its own. Simple sentences have one clause. EXAMPLE: The cat sat on the mat. Complex sentences have a main clause and a subordinate clause. EXAMPLE: The cat sat on the mat, licking its paws. Compound sentences have two clauses joined by a conjunction. EXAMPLE: The cat sat and chewed its tail.
simile	A sentence or group of words which compares something to something else. EXAMPLE: He was as free as a bird.
singular	One of something.
slogan	A sentence or group of words which aims to grab our attention. EXAMPLE: slip, slap, slop
speech marks	The inverted commas that go around what is actually said in direct speech. EXAMPLE: "I want my teddy," said the little boy.
stage directions	Words, phrases or sentences in a playscript which tell actors how to behave or speak.
statement	A type of sentence which tells us something. EXAMPLE: I am called Jane. One of four sentence types.
subordinate clause	See **clause**
suffix	An ending that is added to a word. A suffix can change a word from singular to plural (EXAMPLE: box/box**es**); can change the tense of a verb (EXAMPLE: jump/jump**ed**) or can change the function of a word (EXAMPLE: teach/teach**er**).
summary	A short piece of writing which contains the important points from a longer piece.
tense, past tense, present tense, future tense	Tense tells us when something is happening. Past tense: Something has already happened. EXAMPLE: I **sat** down. I **was sitting** down. Present tense: Something is happening now. EXAMPLE: She **is sitting** down. She **sits** down. Future tense: Something which will happen. EXAMPLE: She **will sit** down.
title	The heading which tells us what the writing is about.
verb	A verb is a word or phrase that tells us what people are doing or being. EXAMPLE: The girls **ran** away. A verb phrase may have a main verb and auxiliary verbs. EXAMPLE: The car **can be** washed after the trip. 'Can' and 'be' are auxiliary verbs. 'Washed' is the main verb.

OXFORD
UNIVERSITY PRESS

Great Clarendon Street, Oxford, OX2 6DP

Oxford University Press is a department of the University of Oxford and furthers the University's aim of excellence in research, scholarship, and education by publishing worldwide in

Oxford New York

Athens Auckland Bangkok Bogotá Buenos Aires Cape Town
Chennai Dar es Salaam Delhi Florence Hong Kong Istanbul Karachi
Kolkata Kuala Lumpur Madrid Melbourne Mexico City Mumbai Nairobi
Paris São Paolo Shanghai Singapore Taipei Tokyo Toronto Warsaw

and associated companies in Berlin Ibadan

Oxford is a registered trade mark of Oxford University Press

British Library Cataloguing in Publication Data

Data available

Illustrated by: Tim Clarey, Kate Davies, Nick Hawken, Bethan Matthews, Uwe Mayer, Shelagh McNicholas, Patricia Moffett, Wendy Sinclair and Mike Spoor

Photographs by: National Library of Jamaica (p6),Popperfoto (p37), Sally Anne Thompson/Animal Photography (p46-47), Corbis Uk Ltd (p51 top right), Image Bank (p51 bottom left), Oxford Scientific Films/A Bailey (p69), Robert Opie Collection (p71).

Cover photograph by: Stock File

Acknowledgements
We are grateful to the following for permission to reproduce copyright material in this book.
Bloomsbury Publishing plc for extracts from *Roar: Animal Rights Handbook for Kids* by Peter Hoggarth (1996); Channel Four Learning for extracts from *Mary Seacole* by Christine Moorcroft and Magnus Magnusson (1998); Devon County Council Environment Department for extracts from Devon Recycling leaflet 'How You can Reduce Your Waste'; Egmont Children's Books Limited, London, for extract from *War Horse* by Michael Morpurgo (first published by Kaye & Ward, 1984); Kingfisher Publications Plc for extract from *The Kingfisher Book of How Things Work* by Steve Parker, copyright © Grisewood & Dempsey 1990, all rights reserved; London Evening Standard via Solo Syndication Ltd for article 'Tails fan anti-docking debate' by Peter Gruner from Evening Standard, 9 March 1999; William Oxley for 'A Modern Witch' first published in Poetry 3 edited by Moira Andrews (Macmillan, 1987), to be published in *Firework Planet* by William Oxley (Acumen Publications, 2000); Oxford University Press for extracts from *Macbeth*, Oxford School Shakespeare edited by Roma Gill (1988); and extracts from Bridget and Neil Ardley: *The Oxford Children's A-Z of the Human Body* (1996); Penguin Books Ltd for extract from *Carrie's War* by Nina Bawden (Puffin, 1974), copyright © Nina Bawden 1973; and for extract from *Goodnight Mr Tom* by Michelle Magorian (Kestrel, 1981), copyright © Michelle Magorian 1981;The Random House Group Ltd for front cover of Boy & Going Solo by Roald Dahl (Omnibus edition, Jonathan Cape 1992); Usborne Publishing for extracts from Richard Dungworth and Philippa Wingate: *Famous Women from Nefertiti to Thatcher* (1997); and from 'Mother Seacole's Balaclava Boys' from Paul Dowswell: *Tales of Real Heroism* (1996).

ISBN 0 19 915553 4

Printed in Hong Kong